APPLAUSE
CHINESE BUSINESS

"ONE OF THE STARS OF THE CH
SUBSTANTIAL CONTRIBUTION TO ALL OF HIS FELLOW TEAM MEMBERS. With this book as a guide, the average businessman might just win one for the Gipper. . . . Important fundamentals . . . clear explanations . . . humorous . . . comprehensive . . . a welcome introduction to the rhythm and grace of Chinese social interaction."

—*Asian Wall Street Journal*

"After watching two decades of China's 'reform and opening,' Seligman's keen eye for both change and continuity will be appreciated by new visitors and old hands alike. A PERCEPTIVE AND COMPREHENSIVE TOUR OF CHINESE MANNERS AND INTERACTIONS WITH FOREIGNERS."

—Douglas Murray, president, National Committee on U.S.-China Relations

"Takes the myth and mystery out of doing business in the modern-day Middle Kingdom. . . . Goes way beyond the rites and rituals of doing business in China to explore the way your Chinese business partner or negotiating adversary thinks and must operate to survive in his own system."

—James McGregor, chief representative, China, Dow Jones & Co., and former president of the American Chamber of Commerce in China

"ESSENTIAL . . . PRACTICAL, INFORMED, BALANCED . . . Scott Seligman knows China and the Chinese."

—Jerome A. Cohen, resident partner (Hong Kong office), Paul, Weiss, Rifkind, Wharton & Garrison, Attorneys at Law

"RELEVANT . . . POWERFUL . . . FASCINATING . . . a wealth of useful information. . . . Provides readers with a wider social context, making at times compelling reading. . . . An accessible and thorough reference book that will do much to reassure the foreign businessman."

—*Far East Business*

more . . .

"VALUABLE, IN FACT, ESSENTIAL. . . . Its clear and concise prose leaves the reader well prepared and eager for an encounter with the Chinese—on their turf!"

—David B. Warner, senior vice president, ChinaVest Limited, and former general manager, China/Hong Kong/South Asia, First National Bank of Chicago

"USEFUL . . . NOT JUST FOR FIRST-TIMERS. . . . Instills a sense of comfort and camaraderie. . . . Level-headed . . . informed, unpretentious, and often funny."

—Business Traveller

"Leads the reader through both the logistical and cultural hazards. . . . His insights will prove AS VALUABLE FOR THE EXPERIENCED CHINA HAND AS FOR THE FIRST-TIME VISITOR."

—Arthur Rosen, president emeritus, National Committee on U.S.-China Relations

"Sensible . . . useful . . . Seligman certainly knows his way around China and the Chinese. He knows, too, how to deal with the 2,500 years of etiquette that faces those hoping to break into Chinese life and business. . . . SELIGMAN WRITES IN AN EASY, COMPREHENSIBLE STYLE, LACING HIS ADMONITIONS WITH CONSIDERABLE WIT."

—South China Morning Post

"WISE, CHARMING, PRACTICAL, AND COMPREHENSIVE . . . the definitive guide to bridging U.S.-China cultural barriers. Seligman's witty and measured style bears witness to his own mastery of the formidable patience, fair-mindedness, and good humor necessary to successful dealings with China. . . . No neophyte should go to China unarmed with this book."

—Judith Shapiro, coauthor, *Son of the Revolution* and *After the Nightmare*

CHINESE BUSINESS ETIQUETTE

A GUIDE TO PROTOCOL, MANNERS, AND CULTURE IN THE PEOPLE'S REPUBLIC OF CHINA

SCOTT D. SELIGMAN

Foreword by Robert A. Kapp, president, United States-China Business Council

Illustrations by Edward J. Trenn

NEW YORK BOSTON

To the memory of my father,
William R. Seligman
(1918–1997)

Warner Business Books
Warner Books

Time Warner Book Group
1271 Avenue of the Americas, New York, NY 10020
Visit our Web site at www.twbookmark.com.

Printed in the United States of America

First Printing: March 1999

10 9 8 7 6

Library of Congress Cataloging-in-Publication Data

Seligman, Scott D.
Chinese business etiquette : a guide to protocol, manners, and culture in the People's Republic of China / Scott D. Seligman.
p. cm.
Rev. ed. of: Dealing with the Chinese. 1989.
Includes index.
ISBN 0-446-67387-0
1. China—Social life and customs—1976– 2. Business etiquette—China. 3. Corporations, Foreign—China. I. Seligman, Scott D. Dealing with the Chinese. II. Title. III. Title: Guide to protocol and manners in the People's Republic of China.
DS779.23.S45 1999
306'.0951—DC21 98-6786
CIP

Illustrations by Edward J. Trenn
Interior design by Charles Sutherland

Acknowledgments

I wish, as I did in *Dealing with the Chinese*, the first rendition of this book, to express appreciation to eight very special people who have, over a period of about twenty-five years, done the most to shape my thinking about the profound differences—and striking similarities—between Chinese and Westerners, and without whom this book could not possibly have been written: Lisa Chang Ahnert, the late Robert C. Atmore, I-Chuan Chen, Li Wenda, Christopher H. Phillips, Ivor N. Shepherd, Roger W. Sullivan, and Ruth Weiss.

Thanks are due also to the following people for their unselfish assistance in the creation of *Dealing with the Chinese*: Edward Ahnert, Carolyn Brehm, Simon Chen, Marsha Cohan, Ellen Eliasoph, Jean Hoffman, Dale Hoiberg, Sara Kane, Lester Lau, Jennifer Little, Chris Lonsdale, Stephen Markscheid, Jeffrey Schultz, Lida Wagner, and Suzher Yan.

Others helped in the creation of *Chinese Business Etiquette* by reviewing new material and sharing experiences that helped illustrate some central concepts. In particular, I'd like to thank Martin Alintuck, Curtis Chin, John Donaldson, Stephanie Hallford, John Holden, Jamie Horsley, Melinda Long, Jim McGregor, Freda Murck, Ted Plafker, Michael Primont, Elyse Silverberg, Anne Stevenson-Yang, Mia Turner, Rebecca Weiner, and Bell Yung.

Contents

Preface

IN THE DECADE SINCE *DEALING WITH THE CHINESE* WAS FIRST published, interacting with the Chinese has become increasingly like interacting with nationals from most other countries. As China bounds headlong into the twenty-first century at a pace hitherto unknown in its history, and sloughs off its Leninist skin for good in favor of its own peculiar coat of "socialism with Chinese characteristics," the influence of the West—in technology, but also in culture and manners—is more and more keenly felt.

For example, when *Dealing with the Chinese* was written in 1988, mainland Chinese really did still refer to each other as *tongzhi*, which means "comrade." In the late 1990s, by contrast, when this term is employed at all, it is generally used either sarcastically or to describe an old revolutionary who has just died. A decade ago it would have been an unpardonable slight not to send a welcoming party to the airport to receive a visiting foreign business delegation; today, in all but extremely high-level visits, doing this has become the exception rather than the rule. In the first book I warned those hosting Chinese visitors in their home countries to eschew hamburgers and pizza in favor of more Chinese-style fare; this was, however, before the conquest of the People's Republic of China (PRC) market by McDonald's, Pizza Hut, and Domino's and the ecumenical effects they have wreaked on the Chinese palate.

None of this means that the old rules no longer govern. The Chinese have not become Americans overnight, nor will they ever become so, no matter how many joint ventures they establish or how many of their children undertake graduate study in the West. Not even the Taiwanese or the Hong Kong Chinese, who are arguably two or three decades further along the Westernization curve than their mainland brethren, have scrapped their Chinese values, norms, attitudes, or rules of conduct. What they have done is to adapt to a rapidly changing environment. And adaptation generally means changing not only observable behavior, but, ultimately, also perceptions, attitudes, and expectations as well.

What all of this *does* mean is that it is getting rarer and rarer to find a Chinese entirely untouched by at least some foreign values and behavior patterns. It means that fewer people, especially urban Chinese, fit old stereotypical profiles, and one now finds examples—sometimes pervasive, sometimes isolated—of Western thinking and behavior in even the most traditional of Chinese people. The truth is, being Chinese is coming more and more to imply incorporating some formerly Western, and now increasingly universal, values, attitudes, and practices. At a minimum, as more Chinese get a taste of Western values, they become more understanding and forgiving of Western manners when they encounter them.

The problem is, one can't count on being so indulged in any given situation. Chinese still view the world through Chinese lenses, and most can't help but look askance at those who deviate from accepted norms. Conversely, they are impressed and flattered when foreigners do things "the right way"—that is, *their* way. Understanding what the Chinese expect and why they expect it is still, therefore, vitally important to all who wish to deal with them. In most cases it continues to make the crucial difference between success and failure. It remains the goal of this book.

I have had the good fortune to spend the last three years in China—my first extended period of residence here since the early 1980s. I had traveled to the PRC many times in the interim, and so I was not unaware of the profound changes that have occurred in the Chinese social fabric, but it took relocating to China for me to understand them in more than a superficial way.

My work in a joint venture has permitted me to view firsthand the commingling of—and conflicts between—the Chinese and Western approaches to business and life. That the joint venture felt very Chinese to my Western colleagues and me but struck our Chinese colleagues as unmistakably foreign seems to me to speak volumes. The young, English-speaking Chinese with whom I worked have proven able teachers. They kept me current on how they view the world and what is and isn't true about today's China. In many cases, it's quite a jump from the China I knew fifteen years ago.

New China, however, remains very much a work in progress, and while some of the rules of the past continue to apply, the norms and values that govern are by all measures a rapidly moving target. To remain useful to foreigners who wish to deepen their understanding of China, therefore, the book needed a good dusting off.

Chinese Business Etiquette is the revised version, rewritten not only to take into account the profound changes of the last decade, but also to reflect a deeper understanding of some traditional Chinese constructs—like *mianzi*, (face) and *guanxi* (connections)—that I have been privileged to acquire over the last several years. It is my sincere hope that it will remain useful for many years to come.

Scott D. Seligman
Beijing

Foreword by Robert A. Kapp

WHETHER IT IS AIRPLANE READING ON THE FIRST TRIP TO China or late-night hotel brush-up reading on the fiftieth business trip, *Chinese Business Etiquette* sets a high standard for a reader-friendly, business-useful guide to the behavioral labyrinth that Americans and other Westerners encounter in China.

This book demystifies much of what otherwise might baffle and intimidate foreigners at work or play in China. It renders normal what might otherwise seem dauntingly exotic. It gives nervous first-timers enough of a sense of what to expect that they will not be bowled over when they encounter it. It provides reassurance to readers that their experiences in China are most likely not unique, and certainly not mainly caused by the reader's particularities. But in the end, no matter how many times we consult *Chinese Business Etiquette* before, during, or after an "action" in China, there will be new insights to glean, new ideas to share with this lively author and his lively book. *Chinese Business Etiquette* will never render itself obsolete.

What this book manages so happily to do is tread the fine line between necessary generalization and treacherous caricature. Americans and Chinese often start with a certain "They all look alike" approach to one another. It is amusing, if dismaying, to find generation after generation of well-established Americans "discovering" that despite names that "sound the same" and black hair and other shared features, the Chinese people "aren't all alike after all." The same thing happens the other way around; I know from experience.

Scott Seligman has studied and lived in China long enough to distill many of the key shared behavioral characteristics that Chinese people generally display, without falling into overly gross generalizations about "them." China, as anyone who has spent time there knows, has its "ways." The old American pop culture phrase about "Confucius say," despite its racist linguistic parody, was rooted in a real phenomenon, the fact that China "has an old saying" for just about any human situation imaginable.

The blackboard of Chineseness, in spite of Mao Zedong's characterization of the impoverished Chinese masses as "poor and blank," has never been empty. The geographer Rhoads Murphey, writing three decades ago about the historic dilemmas of China's modernization, noted that China never suffered through an identity crisis ("Who are we?") as it faced the unfamiliar cultural and material challenge of the modern West. To the contrary, the Chinese never doubted for a moment who they were. The problem of modernity, Murphey noted, sprang more from the fact that the Chinese, so comfortably rooted in China's established cultural system, found the setbacks and defeats of the nineteenth and early twentieth centuries utterly discordant with the accustomed norms that went with being Chinese in the first place. Seligman is on solid ground in portraying widely shared and long-inherited behavioral norms, rooted in truly ancient Chinese customs and traditions.

While Seligman has excelled in these broad and interpretive introductions of essential aspects of contemporary Chinese human relations and behavior, he helps us to understand that one of those enduring norms is what I might call the "power of situational specificity."

Much of what a foreigner encounters in China is neither totally standardized cookie-cutter behavior nor the utterly unique, for-you-and-you-alone response that Americans raised on a diet of individual self-expression yearn for when visiting or working in China. Americans are sometimes dismayed to discover that they are in fact receiving "Foreign Guest/American/Male/Middle-aged" or "Foreigner/Intellectual/China Novice/Young" treatment by their Chinese counterparts. This is what I mean by the power of situational specificity.

As Seligman conveys, the core concepts of classical Chinese philosophy, which have percolated down through 2,500 or more years of essentially continuous civilization, revolve around human relationships. Notwithstanding the arrival of modern nationalism and Marxist-Leninist social revolution in the present century, these norms of human behavior have never been eradicated. And at the center of these norms is the idea that right behavior is situationally appropriate: that proper behavior toward one's elders is different from that toward one's juniors, that parents must behave "parentally" toward their offspring while their offspring must demonstrate "filial piety" toward their parents, that one's closest loyalties are to close family in all situations. And that, to take the focal issues of Seligman's book, "foreign guests" are to be treated in certain ways because they are foreign guests.

In the past, I often briefed delegations of educated and professionally prominent Americans preparing to visit China for the first time. I found from my own lengthening experience in China that they needed to know the following: On about the eleventh day of a three-week visit, someone in the group would look at the fourteen-dish luncheon staring him in the face, suddenly become pale, and announce in a choking voice, "I want a watercress salad," or "I have got to have a peanut butter–and-jelly sandwich or I may lose my self-control." I tried to reassure the travelers, who usually looked at me with some suspicion, that an incident like this was normal and predictable, but that it would do no good to wallow around in the bathos of it.

The mini-rebellion against yet another fourteen-dish luncheon, I suggested, was the first sign of real understanding of what it means to be in China. The fact was, I pointed out, that foreign guests got fourteen-dish lunches because they were Foreign Guests. That is, the category "Foreign Guest" brought with it a whole set of situationally required forms of treatment, one of which was huge meals. That the guest wanted a peanut butter sandwich instead was really not the point; foreign guests get Foreign Guest treatment.

The second meaning of the Peanut Butter Rebellion Syndrome, though, was somewhat deeper, and touches on what makes Scott Seligman's book so rewarding and useful. The Americans' frustration over the luncheon menu, in my view, expressed a deeper uneasiness that one simply has to manage and deal with if one is to function effectively in China.

That uneasiness is that China really is bigger than we are. That no matter how impressive any particular person—foreign or Chinese, for that matter—might be, no matter how significant an "achiever" one might know oneself to be from all those triumphs at Harvard or General Consolidated Amalgamated Enterprises or from the law review or the hotshot legislative staffer's inside track, none of that matters a whole lot in China. Americans discover to their dismay that the route to effectiveness in China lies not in demonstrations of individual brilliance or pyrotechnics, but rather in mastering the unfamiliar requirements of situational specificity.

The bad news is that, for many Americans, this is uncomfortable and arduous. Why say the same thing that everybody else says on set-piece occasions? Isn't that a repression of personality, a rejection of one's own dignity? In the end, isn't acting in accordance with the externally defined situational requirement simply foolish?

Not if it works.

The good news, as Scott Seligman's book makes so seriously and amusingly clear, is that acting in accordance with the requirements of highly nuanced but seldom unique situations is a learnable skill. You don't have to be born in China to learn it. You don't have to be ethnically Chinese to learn it. You don't have to know the Chinese language to learn it. You don't have to have a Ph.D. to learn it. You're not at a fatal disadvantage in learning it just because you're one of those straight-shooting, no-nonsense Americans that most Americans think themselves to be.

In any cross-cultural encounter, there is plenty of room for simple, untrained warmth and good will, calm dignity, and the kind of broad acceptance of shared humanity that can link human beings together in any time or any place. But, in my view, good will and a kind of misty affirmation of the brotherhood/sisterhood of humankind is seldom sufficient to ensure satisfying and rewarding engagements with our Chinese friends and colleagues.

Neither is a starting belief that because, in some theological sense, every individual (Chinese or non-Chinese) is completely unique, no generalizations at all—no broad guidelines to Chinese human relations situations whatever—can ever apply.

Chinese Business Etiquette is a primer, a guide, and a refresher course for all of us as we strive to improve our effectiveness in dealing with Chinese counterparts on their home soil. As I approach my fortieth visit to China, more than two decades after I made my first trip, I am glad that I have Seligman close at hand. He, through this wonderful book, is the perfect traveling and business companion.

入境而问禁
入国而问俗
入门而问讳

"If you enter a region, ask what its prohibitions are;
if you visit a country, ask what its customs are;
if you cross a family's threshold, ask what its taboos are."

—From *Li Ji* (*The Book of Rites*)
One of the five Confucian classics,
circa 500 B.C.

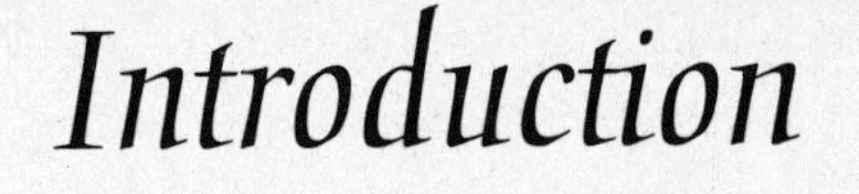

Introduction

The Scrutable Chinese

YOUR COMPANY HAS JUST SIGNED AN IMPORTANT JOINT VENTURE agreement with a Chinese corporation, and it's up to you to plan the signing ceremony. You decide to err on the side of caution and include on the guest list everyone who has been involved in the negotiations, including two individuals from the same government ministry. One has been a staunch friend of your company since the very beginning, and her active involvement kept the talks on track more than once when thorny problems presented themselves. The second, her boss, has been involved only peripherally.

To honor this woman and thank her for her help, you make sure your CEO recognizes her personally in his remarks. For some reason, however, on the night of the event both she and her boss appear to be extremely subdued, and you think you even detect an undertone of antagonism. Did you do something wrong? And if so, what can you do to make things right?

Perhaps you are the guest of honor at a banquet with a vice minister of an important government ministry. It is the first time you have met the man, and you are eager to make a good impression on him, since his support will be crucial to the success of an agreement your company hopes to conclude. The waiter brings a plate of food to the table, and the vice minister enthusiastically piles your tiny dish high with sea slug, which he assures you is a delicacy in China and very nourishing. You look at the dull, brownish rubbery substance and feel an unmistakable gag welling up in your throat. What do you do? Can you refuse it without causing offense?

At a similar banquet given by the managing director of a state-owned corporation in a provincial capital, the host raises a glass of fiery *Maotai* liquor and challenges you to down the contents of your glass in one gulp. Everyone at the table exhorts you to try, and you get the distinct impression that a refusal will call your masculinity into question. But you're quite sure the 106-proof beverage will burn a hole in your stomach. Is the contract worth a night of severe discomfort in your hotel room? Do you have any other choices?

Or maybe you are hurrying down the stairs of a department store in Taipei or Shanghai and you suddenly lose your footing. You slip down most of a flight of stairs and find yourself on your backside looking up at a crowd of a dozen or more Chinese shoppers. No one lifts a hand to help you, and as you study the faces in the crowd, you detect unmistakable mirth on many of them. As the laughter continues, you feel like killing someone. After all, you could have been badly hurt. Why did this happen? And what does it mean?

These are just a few examples of cross-cultural situations that simply cannot be taken at face value if they are to be interpreted properly. If you find yourself in one of them, you may feel absolutely certain you have been wronged or embarrassed, or you may feel completely perplexed at a sudden turn of events. Sometimes it's only a minor misunderstanding, but other times a lot rides on your ability to divine what is going on and formulate an appropriate response. Like a valued friendship. Or a multimillion-dollar business deal.

That's exactly what this book is all about. Why do the Chinese behave as they do? What do their sometimes bewildering actions or pronouncements really mean? How can you figure out what motivates them when they conduct business? What are the predictable areas in which their cultural norms are most likely to collide with those of Westerners? And how can you learn to deal effectively with them?

Anyone engaged in business with the Chinese or considering doing business in China should find this book useful. This includes people traveling to the People's Republic of China (PRC) for brief negotiations as well as those posted in China for extended periods, whether as business representatives, technicians, diplomats, or scholars. Casual tourists, even on a short stay in China, are also likely to find the book worthwhile, and will probably understand a good deal more of what goes on around them as a result of reading it.

Most of the examples in the book concentrate on life in the PRC, but anyone planning to travel to Taiwan, the Hong Kong Special Administrative Region (SAR), Macao, or even Singapore on business or pleasure should also find this book of interest, since the similarities among Chinese living on the mainland and many of those who reside in other places greatly outweigh the differences. And finally, the book should also prove useful as a guide for people involved in hosting Chinese groups visiting their own country.

The book is organized according to substantive areas, with some general discussions of cultural differences and intercultural relationships (Chapters 1, 4, and 7, for example) as well as specific points relating to important situations such as meetings, banquets, gift-giving, negotiations, and hosting. The most important points to remember about each major topic are summarized in a recap section at the end of each chapter.

My own credentials for writing this book consist primarily of experience in mainland China, Taiwan, and Hong Kong that spans twenty-five years, including a total of eight years of residence in these places. What has always intrigued me most about the Chinese are the cultural differences between them and the Westerners with whom they have relationships and do business. These are sometimes profound and sometimes trivial, and most often somewhere in between. How we perceive one another, and how we can learn to bridge the gaps and communicate clearly, has always held a strong fascination for me.

One final credential to which I'd like to own up is an abiding affection and respect for the Chinese people. I say this not to warn the reader of a potential bias in favor of the Chinese in the following pages, but rather to mitigate against what might otherwise seem at times to be quite the opposite. This book may appear in places to be critical of the Chinese and their practices, and I certainly don't spare them their lumps when and where I feel they deserve them, for it seems to me that to do any less would be to write a book that is less than candid, and hence misleading to the reader. But in truth, I could not have lasted in this business this long if I were not energized and charmed by my interactions with Chinese people. I hope this book will help others to feel the same way.

One of the old saws concerning writing about China—at least China in the late twentieth century—is that the situation usually changes before the ink has had a chance to dry on the page. This has been the consistent finding of all who presume to commit to paper their observations about Chinese politics. Movements have come and gone with great rapidity in the last three decades, and no matter what one writes, one's words are invariably overtaken by events. Those who try to provide guidance on doing business in China generally find that even before the page proofs come back from the publisher, the cast of characters has changed, or a new law, regulation, or policy has been promulgated that makes an entire chapter irrelevant if not inaccurate.

This constant and rapid evolution is much less the case in the area of culture, protocol, and etiquette, which is considerably less vulnerable to the winds of change than business or politics. China may be changing rapidly, but patterns of interaction among people have by and large been affected as little by the 1949 revolution and the 1979 reopening to the outside world as they were by the upheavals of 2,500 years of history. Beneath a thin veneer of socialist ideology and communist practice, Chinese interactions are governed by patterns laid down and developed through the experience of thousands of years. Business practices may become more sophisticated, and material goods may flow in from the West, but the underlying principles of human interaction tend to be very resistant to change.

Manners evolve, too, of course, but they do so somewhat more slowly than other things. And one of the happy characteristics of etiquette is that one is seldom faulted for conservatism. Following traditionally acceptable practices could conceivably cause you to appear old-fashioned, but it will never put you at risk of committing a faux pas.

Still, things do change, and Chinese protocol has changed since the publication of *Dealing with the Chinese*. In preparing this book, I've taken care to ensure that it is as up-to-date as possible. The majority of situations, attitudes, and practices discussed are undoubtedly timeless as far as the Chinese are concerned. The use of *guanxi*—connections—isn't likely to lose its tremendous importance in the foreseeable future, nor are the Chinese likely to abandon their fixation with the concept of *mianzi*, or face. And I'd give odds that a dozen years from now, business meetings in China will be conducted in a fashion quite similar to the format used today.

Nonetheless, the reader is strongly encouraged to use the book as a guide rather than a mandate or prescription. If a suggested path of action doesn't get the desired result, or if an interpretation of someone else's behavior doesn't seem to ring true, by all means try something else. Good manners is generally just good common sense anyway. The purpose of this book is precisely to shed some light and to contribute some insight as to exactly what it is that constitutes "good common sense" when Westerners deal with the increasingly scrutable Chinese.

Protocol and the Larger Picture

2,500 Years of Interpersonal Relationships

THOUGH KEENLY AWARE OF THEIR NEED TO LEARN FROM THE West in technological areas in which their country lags behind the rest of the world, the Chinese people have never felt the need for instruction from outsiders in the areas of decorum and protocol. Since Confucius codified the universe of interpersonal relationships and their associated duties nearly 2,500 years ago, the Chinese have had an established set of principles governing etiquette on which they have always been able to rely.

China has historically been a highly homogeneous society with little tolerance for deviation from generally accepted norms of behavior. To most Chinese there are proper and improper ways for people to behave toward one another, and you will seldom hear much argument as to exactly what these are. Precisely because they tend to share a set of assumptions about how to act, the Chinese are fond of lecturing one another about what constitutes proper behavior in a given situation. There are relatively few gray areas, even in what is becoming an increasingly complex society.

This being said, however, it is important to point out that the Chinese generally hold only other Chinese to all of these exacting standards. Disparagement that may readily be directed toward an erring fellow countryman is not as likely to be leveled at a foreigner. On the contrary; the body of knowledge concerning proper behavior is greatly revered and not considered to be easily acquired; no one who was not raised Chinese can reasonably be expected ever to master it completely.

The Chinese are probably correct in this last assertion. You'll never be as Chinese as the Chinese; in fact, if you were not born Chinese, you'll never be Chinese at all, no matter how much you understand about them. But this does not mean that it doesn't pay to try to learn their ways. Even if you accept the fact that a foreigner will never really "measure up" to the often subtle standards of protocol held by most Chinese, there are nonetheless considerable benefits to be derived by trying to master the art.

THE ADVANTAGES OF LEARNING CHINESE WAYS

Learning Chinese customs is worthwhile for a number of reasons. First of all, it is useful because imitation is the sincerest form of flattery, even to the Chinese. You'll score a lot of points with a Chinese friend or business associate if you remember to use both hands when you offer your business card or to turn your chopsticks around and use the thicker end when serving food to others during a meal. Even if you never become a latter-day Confucian, you'll ingratiate yourself by demonstrating a sincere desire to make your counterpart comfortable with you. The Chinese are quite simply delighted when foreigners try to speak with them in their own language—even if it is badly mangled—or deal with them according to their own rules.

Then too, there is the benefit of understanding more clearly what is going on around you. Even if *you* don't play by Chinese rules, *they* always do. They will give subtle signals that express how they feel throughout their interaction with you. Since these are, for the most part, cues not commonly understood by Westerners, many of them will be incomprehensible to the uninitiated. It's up to you whether you choose to acquire the tools to interpret them or not.

Knowing the meaning of these cues can give you a distinct advantage in business and even social situations. It can help you understand whether you have offended, pleased, flattered, or amused someone, backed someone into a corner, or caused him or her to lose face. It can help you divine the nature of the relationship between two Chinese people—who defers to whom, who outranks whom, and who really makes the decisions. And it can help you determine what you need to do to keep things moving in the right direction.

Dealing with the Chinese does not necessarily mean playing entirely by their rules, however. Intercultural communication is a two-way street, and there should always be give-and-take on both sides. In fact, it's a mistake when visiting China to attempt slavishly to do as the Chinese do and forget your own cultural values in the process. You'll be uncomfortable and unsure of yourself, and unlikely to be able to conceal this fact from your hosts. And you'll be ceding all advantage to your counterparts, who, after all, will always understand the rules better than you do.

What you are left with, then, is a tightrope of sorts. It's advisable to learn how to see relationships and obligations through Chinese eyes, because understanding how they view a situation provides definite advantages. It's also flattering to attempt to do as the Chinese do, and they will certainly appreciate the gesture. But it's equally important to remember who *you* are and what cultural baggage *you* bring to the party. The Chinese may not be interested in changing the way they do things, but unless they are provoked or they feel that something of overriding importance is at stake, they can generally be counted on to try to make you comfortable with them. It's precisely the converse—learning enough about them to make them comfortable with you—that one wants to strive for here.

Taiwan, Hong Kong, and the Mainland

Although this book is written specifically with the People's Republic of China (PRC) in mind, much of what is contained herein is applicable to Chinese living elsewhere in the world. Chinese people reared entirely in foreign cultures, such as American-born Chinese, are quite likely to have more in common with their fellow countrymen than they do with China mainlanders or Taiwanese. But it is probably fair to say that there are more commonalities than there are differences among the majority of Chinese in the world.

The bulk of the Chinese people who live outside of mainland China today are relatively recent emigrants—by Chinese standards, anyway—whose families left the mainland within the last one or two hundred years. A high percentage live in Taiwan, Hong Kong, Macao, and Singapore, as well as in Malaysia, Indonesia, the Philippines, and other countries of Southeast Asia. Many others live in the United States, Canada, Australia, Europe, and even Latin America. Asian Chinese in particular tend to share more cultural values with their compatriots on the mainland, and those in Hong Kong, Macao, and Taiwan undoubtedly share the most. The differences that do exist are far more likely to stem from politics than from culture.

For example, a person in Taiwan would be unlikely to feel bound by communist-inspired restrictions concerning the nature or value of gifts he may or may not receive from a business associate, but his or her behavior after a gift is offered—obligatory refusal and repeated protestations—might well be indistinguishable from that of a mainland compatriot. Seating arrangements at a banquet in Hong Kong might owe a little less to strict organizational protocol and a little more to informal friendships, but the order of the dishes and the ritual of toasting might well be lifted right out of a Beijing event. And the setting for a business meeting in Singapore might be a modern office rather than a stuffy meeting room, but the guest of honor would still very likely be placed on the host's right—just as he or she might in China or indeed, in Hong Kong or Taiwan.

This is not to say that communism has not made its mark on Chinese social attitudes, or that people in the PRC don't do certain things differently. The Cultural Revolution of 1966–1976 had devastating effects on interpersonal relationships that are felt even to this day. Chinese in the PRC who lived through this period tend to be less trusting and friendly toward people they do not know and less likely to express unorthodox opinions in their presence than younger Chinese. And while the Chinese have historically been a group-centered people, the amount of social control held by one's work unit over one's life in the PRC (see Chapter 4) is unprecedented in Chinese history, except perhaps by that once enjoyed by the patriarch of the extended family. Happily, the demise of the tyranny of the *danwei* (work unit; see Chapter 4) is one of the effects of the changes that have shaped China since 1979.

Throughout this book, differences the reader is likely to encounter in Taiwan, Hong Kong, and Southeast Asia will be pointed out. What is perhaps most surprising is, after you scratch the surface, how few significant ones you really find.

Chapter II

Getting in Touch

ONCE, EARLY IN MY CHINA CAREER, I RECEIVED A TELEPHONE call from someone at an American company that had done no business in the PRC, but was interested in developing some. It was clear from the sound of his voice that the man was extremely frazzled and frustrated. He had been put in charge of developing the China market and was eager to succeed. He had done his research and identified a Chinese organization he felt would be a fitting business partner for his firm. He had drafted a telex to that unit (the preferred form of communication in those days), putting forth an abbreviated business proposition, and had sent it off to China. When he received no response, he reconfirmed the telex number and tried again. And again. When I spoke with him four telexes later, he was just about to wash his hands of the whole idea.

We'll never know for sure exactly what the problem was, but I'd put money on something approximating the following scenario: All of the telexes were of course received by the Chinese unit, and after translation they made their way to the desk of someone fairly responsible in the organization—probably a manager or a director. The name of the company wasn't familiar to the manager, so he asked around a bit but found no one in the unit who had ever heard of this company.

Perhaps one of the unit's translators consulted a reference book on U.S. businesses but couldn't identify the company, or perhaps there was an error in spelling or in translation. Or perhaps no one even took the matter that far. In any event, once it was clear no one had ever heard of the company, the leader decided not to risk taking any further action. And once that decision was made, repeated telexes were just a waste of time, money, and paper.

It wouldn't happen the same way today, of course. Chinese corporations are far more independent of government bureaucracies these days, and more aggressive about doing business abroad. In fact, someone today might be far more vulnerable to criticism for letting a potential deal slip through his or her fingers than for taking a chance on a new, untested partner. But the difficulty in this situation—that since no one had any knowledge of the foreign company, no one could vouch for its worthiness as a business partner—underscores a basic principle that remains true: The Chinese don't like doing business with strangers or companies of which they've never heard, and ventures and transactions in which precious foreign exchange is at stake are no place for taking unnecessary chances.

There could have been any number of reasons that the American company didn't receive any response at all. First, a negative response is considered impolite; silence communicates the same thing as an overt rebuff, and it is less awkward for all concerned. Second, Chinese generally do not feel social obligations to people or organizations they do not know. The telex was sent by a stranger, and one has no obligation to a stranger. Simply put, the Chinese probably didn't feel they owed anyone an answer. And third, if the manager or some other responsible official in the unit had decided on a course of "no action," no underling would have even thought of taking even the small amount of individual initiative that a polite rebuff would have required.

One thing the company might have done differently would have been to work through an intermediary—that is, some individual or organization known to the Chinese unit who might make the formal introduction and, in so doing, vouch for the reliability of the company. It might be a consultant or consulting firm, a business partner, an embassy representative, or simply an acquaintance. Going through an intermediary can build confidence with the Chinese, who even after twenty years of an open-door policy may lack exposure to world-famous companies and behave as relative newcomers to the modern international business scene. Intermediaries are valuable in interpersonal relationships as well; someone who has been introduced by a trusted friend is automatically deemed worthy of trust.

In part because of this attitude, government organizations in China have always maintained "external affairs" departments designed to serve as intermediaries with foreigners. While at worst these organizations may simply add a layer of bureaucracy between you and your ultimate targets, they can also help open the right doors if you are patient. Using intermediaries from outside the ministry effectively bypasses these offices.

As doing business in China gets more "normal," the need

for go-betweens is diminishing. Now it's easier than ever to make contact yourself. To avoid a nonresponse like the one described above, however, it's best in your initial overture to present a lot of information about your company and the venture that you propose. Send materials that describe your company and its history, and literature about its products or services. And the more Chinese-language materials, the better. Be as specific as you can about the type of business arrangement you wish to discuss, and how and where you propose to meet.

It is probably fair to say that the same thing would not have happened in Hong Kong or Taiwan, because these areas tend to be a great deal more sophisticated in international trade, as any examination of their impressive trade statistics would prove. But even though a Taiwanese businessman would likely have answered the first telex, that doesn't mean that he wouldn't have been more comfortable with more detailed information about the U.S. company, or with the blessing of a trusted intermediary. The fact remains that the Chinese strongly prefer to do business with "old friends." And though this status can be attained relatively quickly and easily after the initial ice is broken—it really just means that some form of relationship, or *guanxi* (see Chapter 10) has been established—without it, the going is often rough at first.

COUNTERPART ORGANIZATIONS

Even though personal relationships—*guanxi*—are vitally important in China (see Chapter 10), business relationships with Chinese organizations are supposed to be institutional in nature. That is, individuals—even if they are instrumental in forging the association—ought to be able to come and go without affecting its basic nature. If General Electric signs an agreement with the Beijing Engine Works, that Chinese unit would likely feel obligated to receive any GE representative courteously; it doesn't have to be the senior vice president who negotiated or initialed the agreement.

Indeed, that particular person may have long since passed from the scene. What is supposed to live on is the relationship between the corporations. Personal relationships live on, too, of course, and when individuals switch units they carry with them all of the contacts from their previous working lives. But what is important to note here is that institutional relationships are not considered to be predicated on personal relationships alone.

It might have occurred to you that in the example above the failure of the American businessman to direct the telex to any particular individual at the Chinese company was a mistake. In fact, strictly speaking, it was not. Unlike in the West, you generally do not need to deal with a specific individual to do business in the PRC. Leadership is still collective, and historically it has always been the unit—not any individual—that ostensibly holds ultimate authority, though this is changing. This is why a Chinese business letter is far more likely to bear the chop (official seal) of the unit—usually a red, circular stamp—than it is the personal signature of the writer. It's also why an invitation to visit China will generally be issued by an organization, and not by an individual.

None of this means that individuals are not important to business. Organizations are nothing more than collections of individuals, after all, some more resourceful, powerful, and well connected than others. It is always a good idea to cultivate friends in any organization with which you happen to be dealing. Ultimately, it is individuals who make judgments as to whether others are trustworthy business partners, or whether particular deals are advantageous. And the reality is that organizational relationships often *do* change substantially when particular people pass from the scene, just as they do elsewhere.

Nowadays it's relatively easy to get a visa to enter China, and many people come in on tourist visas, without invitations, even to do business. But if you are visiting by invitation, it is still generally issued in the name of a Chinese organization. This unit—it may be a ministry, a corporation, a municipal or provincial government, or a travel service—is known as the host organization, or *jiedai danwei*.

You no longer need a Chinese host organization to arrange for travel within China, book hotels or tickets, or engage in other routine activities. But they remain very useful in running interference for you if you wish to do something out of the ordinary, like arranging a meeting with a state leader or other high official, a visit to a military installation or to some other hard-to-get-into place. And the general rule of thumb is that the more important the host organization is and the higher its prestige, the more pull it is likely to have in getting such things accomplished.

Host organizations are also useful in the early stages of conducting business, and if you wish to explore business opportunities, by all means select a host with influence in your own industry area. Working through the Light Industry Council, for example, makes sense if you are looking for opportunities in the food processing area, since this organization has unparalleled influence and contacts in this field and can open many doors for you. Having a heavy hitter on your side with a stake in making a deal work can be a tremendous advantage in overcoming obstacles. But at the same time, be aware that all Chinese organizations have their own sets of obligations that could lead them to champion their own agendas.

DELEGATIONS

Because their society is so thoroughly group-centered (see Chapter 4), the Chinese are most at ease when dealing with foreign guests in well-organized groups. If you visit China as part of an organized group, regardless of how you and your comrades see yourselves—as a cohesive team, a loosely affiliated assemblage, or even an uncoordinated collection of individuals—the Chinese will see you as a delegation. And delegations take on a life of their own among the Chinese.

Delegations are groups of individuals who bear some relationship to one another—perhaps they all work for the same company, or are all members of the same profession. They are presumed to have a shared purpose, even if it is only to visit Buddhist temples or sample China's finest cuisine. Delegations are generally expected to have some structure, with a leader who makes decisions for the group and some sort of protocol ranking of members. This latter requirement—the need for some ordering of group members—is not so important in tour groups, but it is of some consequence among business delegations.

Above all, delegations are expected to act as groups, and not as random collections of individuals. Nothing confuses and confounds the Chinese more than many voices in a delegation, each expressing a personal opinion as to what the group should do or where it should go. Since consensus is an important component of Chinese group process, they also expect it from foreigners. The delegation is presumed to speak with one voice, and it is the voice of the delegation leader.

Some foreign groups lend themselves to this sort of organization more easily than others. Company delegations fit relatively easily into the mold, with the senior officer generally assuming the duties of the delegation leader. When many different companies are represented on a single industrial delegation, the choice may be harder, and in some cases it may even be totally arbitrary. The selection of the leader is the province of the group members themselves, however; the Chinese will not force their own selection on a group. But if the identity of the leader is not made explicit to them, they may make an inappropriate assumption based on title, or even on a list of delegates they may have received.

You can always tell who it is the Chinese think is in charge. The person understood to be the delegation leader is the person offered the seat of honor to the right at the principal Chinese host in a business meeting or a banquet. Apart from speaking for the group, the delegation leader is also presumed to be responsible for enforcing discipline within the group if it is ever necessary, and for making summary decisions when consensus is difficult to reach.

There are other specific roles in a delegation apart from leadership. When Chinese travel abroad, one person is often designated as liaison to the foreign hosts. This may be the interpreter, whose linguistic facility makes communication easier, but it may also be someone else. It is, however, always someone of rank lower than that of the leader. The liaison isn't responsible for making decisions, but he or she does communicate the wishes of the group to the hosts and vice versa. This person negotiates for the group, passes on requests, expresses criticism or dissatisfaction, and in essence acts for the group leader in potentially difficult or contentious situations.

Naturally, the liaison must get instructions from the leader and clear any course of action before proceeding. By working in this way, the leader is never put in an embarrassing position vis-à-vis his or her hosts, and no loss of face is risked. Negative responses, if they must be expressed at all, are expressed through the liaison.

Organizations that host delegations are expected to assign similar roles to their own individuals. A principal host is assigned to receive any given visiting delegation, and a liaison person is designated as well. Any potentially controversial issues should be negotiated through liaisons, and never raised directly among leaders until they are fully resolved to mutual satisfaction. Leader-to-leader discussions are expected always to be cordial and correct; while liaisons must handle the thorny issues, the leaders remain free to exchange compliments and accolades.

RECAP: SIX POINTS ON GETTING IN TOUCH

1. The Chinese dislike doing business with strangers; it's helpful to be introduced properly by an intermediary known to both sides.
2. Alternatively, if you make an independent initial approach, you should provide as much information as pos-

sible about your company and what you hope to accomplish.

3. Business relationships are institutional in nature and are not necessarily predicated on close personal ties. It's always a good idea to cultivate personal friends in the bureaucracy, however.
4. A host organization is sometimes a helpful thing to have when one visits China. Such organizations should be selected carefully, since your ability to get things accomplished in China often depends on the amount of clout they have in the bureaucracy.
5. Foreign delegations visiting China are expected to coordinate the individual agendas of their members and speak with one voice. They should act as cohesive groups, never random collections of individuals.
6. Delegations have definite structures, and individual members are often assigned specific roles such as leader, interpreter, and liaison. Host organizations also assign similar roles to members of their own staff.

Chapter III

Meeting and Greeting People

MANY WESTERNERS WHO HAVE HAD LITTLE CONTACT WITH the Far East share a common fear that the cultural gaps between China and the West are so vast that bridging them successfully will take a colossal amount of practice and time—if indeed it can be done at all. Such apprehension probably stems far more from the reputation of the Japanese, whose differences from Westerners are really quite a bit more profound than are those of the Chinese. The truth is, though they employ their share of subtle signals that may be difficult to divine, the Chinese are most often friendly, earnest, and enthusiastic communicators.

Count on your Chinese counterpart to be genuinely interested in finding common ground and in learning from you. The fact that you are a foreigner will generally work in your favor. With few exceptions, the Chinese have a natural friendliness toward foreigners, and a natural curiosity about what it is that makes you different from them, though for many the distinction does not go any deeper than "foreigner" versus

"Chinese." That is, only a small percentage of the Chinese you meet care much *which* foreign country you may hail from, and what that might imply about you. It's enough that you are foreign, and hence different from them.

Establishing effective working relations with the Chinese does not require a mastery of the Chinese language, though some knowledge of it—even a few well-chosen words—can generally get you further. The Chinese are flattered when foreigners make an attempt to learn their language, and a phrase or two will certainly earn you high marks. But whether or not you should attempt to conduct a relationship in Chinese depends mostly on your level of proficiency.

If your Mandarin is reasonably good, it's perfectly all right to rattle on in it, though you should be sensitive to the fact that you may be depriving a Chinese friend of a rare opportunity to practice English with a native speaker. If, on the other hand, you have only a few Chinese phrases at your command, it's best to spare everyone the trouble, especially if your counterpart speaks some English. My rule of thumb has always been to speak whichever language makes the conversation flow most easily.

Breaking the Ice

The Chinese prefer to be introduced formally to people they do not know; they are reluctant to strike up chance conversations with strangers. This goes for fellow Chinese as well as foreigners. It's for this reason that conservative Chinese tend to be somewhat uncomfortable attending Western-style cocktail parties, though these pose fewer problems for younger

Chinese and are in fact becoming quite popular in China these days. If you meet someone by chance, you have no way to know anything about the person—what kind of a family he or she comes from, what type of work he or she does, or whether the person is someone worth knowing.

If, on the other hand, a friend introduces you to someone, the new acquaintance is automatically stamped with a seal of approval and deemed worthy of respect and friendship, unless and until he or she proves otherwise. It's as though you have little responsibility to pay any heed at all to strangers, but an implied obligation to be friendly and solicitous to those to whom you have been officially introduced.

While it is always best to have someone present you, this is not absolutely necessary, and you can introduce yourself. If you can cite a common friend at that point, so much the better. But even a simple *Ni hao?* ("How are you?") and a handshake are enough to get you started. Stand up when you are being introduced or are presenting yourself, and stay upright for the duration of the introduction. Say your name and the name of your company or organization if it's relevant, and specify the country that you come from. Speak slowly and distinctly.

Handshakes are the accepted form of greeting in China, even among Chinese. Often, when you are introduced to a group of people, you will be expected to shake hands all around—a bit like hockey teams do at the conclusion of a game. Unlike the Japanese, the Chinese do not greet with a bow at the waist, though if you look carefully you may notice a vestigial nod of the head that takes place when people are introduced to one another or when a handshake occurs.

Present your business card (be sure to have plenty of them with you), making certain to use both hands and grasp the card by two corners in order to be especially polite. Position the card so it is legible to the recipient, and if you have bilingual cards—necessary if you are planning on spending much time in China—make sure the side printed in the person's native language is facing up. When you receive someone's card, spend a few seconds reading it over. This not only helps you remember the name, it also signals respect for the other person. It's impolite to put someone's card directly into your pocket without looking at it first, because this is viewed as demeaning. If it's a sit-down meeting, place the card on the table so you can refer to it.

Initial encounters with the Chinese often follow strikingly similar patterns. When they meet Chinese people for the first time, for example, foreigners visiting China have an excellent chance of being asked one or more of the following "top ten" questions:

Where are you from?
How long have you been in China?
Have you visited China before?
Do you speak Chinese?
What do you think of China?
What kind of work do you do?
Which places in China have you visited?
Are you accustomed to Chinese food?
Are you married?
Do you have any children?

Note that most of these are earnest questions designed to seek out common ground. A lot of Chinese know relatively little about the world beyond the PRC, especially those from outside the major cities, so they will first seek to engage you in conversation concerning something about which they have some knowledge.

Upon learning where you are from, a Chinese will often offer an observation about your country—usually a complimentary one. It may be fairly banal, for example, "Canada is a very large country"; or "We Chinese have a friendly relationship with Australia." Or it may be a comment about a friend or relative who has visited or studied in your country, or a personal account of a trip there.

Don't be surprised if even in an initial encounter you are asked a question or two you deem to be very personal—cultural standards differ here. A Chinese might ask you how much you earn, for example, since salary was traditionally no secret under a communist system in which wages were standardized by rank. (This is beginning to change among the well paid, however, as differences in income grow.) Or you might be asked your age or the cost of something you own or are wearing. If you are single, you might be questioned directly as to why you have not married. Or if you are childless, a Chinese might wonder aloud why you have no children. Chinese people sometimes also comment on physical characteristics that Westerners generally deem off-limits in polite conversation, such as a person's weight, height, baldness, handicap, and so on.

Handle these as best you can. If you object to answering them directly, you can dismiss them with a little humor; a Chinese will rarely pursue such a matter if politely rebuffed in this way. If all else fails, you can explain that in your country one does not normally divulge this type of information, but be sensitive in the way you do this to avoid the impression that the person has committed a major faux pas in your eyes.

Be aware, too, that the knife cuts both ways. Westerners often get too personal too quickly for Chinese tastes, as well. Asking a lot of questions about someone's family, for example—other than the basics of whether someone is married and how many children the person has—can be perceived as inappropriate by a Chinese whom you meet in the course of doing business. Bringing up political issues in such a way as to make a Chinese feel pressed to express an irreverent personal opinion is often unwelcome as well. It's safest to steer clear of politics until you know someone fairly well.

You may find the way in which the Chinese deal with compliments to be rather curious. Accepting praise outright is not considered good etiquette; a Chinese is expected to deflect compliments and pretend he or she is unworthy of receiving them. Try complimenting a Chinese on his or her command of the English language, for example, and you're likely to hear something such as "not at all" or "it isn't really very good" in response.

The Chinese use a number of phrases when flattered, but one of the most common—and by far the most instructive—is *nali*, a word with the literal meaning of the interrogative "where" that in this context is used to mean something such as "It was nothing." (In the Beijing dialect the same idea may be expressed as *nar de hua*.) It's as if to say "The kind words you have just uttered couldn't *possibly* be directed at me! *Where* is the person to whom you are referring?"

Forms of Address: Negotiating Chinese Names

Suppose you have the occasion to meet a Mr. Wang Jianguo. Under no circumstances should he be addressed as Mr.

Jianguo. The first thing you need to remember about Chinese names is that the surname comes *first,* not last. More than 95 percent of all Chinese surnames are one syllable—that is to say, one character—in length; some of the most common examples are Wang, Chen, Zhang, Li, Zhao, and Lin. The remaining few, which are seldom encountered, are two characters in length. Most given names are two syllables long, though it has become increasingly popular on the mainland in recent years to use only one. Thus in the case of Mr. Wang Jianguo, Wang is the surname and Jianguo is the given name. He is properly addressed as Mr. Wang.

When you are speaking Chinese, the surname invariably comes first. But this rule can change if you are speaking English and dealing with Westernized Chinese. Chinese people who are longtime residents of foreign countries, and even some who live in China who have frequent contact with Westerners, occasionally opt to reverse the order of their names—placing the given name first—in order to conform with Western practice and make it easier for their foreign counterparts. So don't be completely surprised if you receive a business card on which someone has thrown you a curve ball and placed his or her given name first. It's rare, but it does happen.

In point of fact, in business situations you will seldom really need to concern yourself with a Chinese person's given name at all, at least not during face-to-face contact. Unlike in the West, where you may call someone by his or her first name shortly after meeting for the first time, in China almost no one is called by the given name alone, except by close relatives or extremely intimate friends of long standing. Even good friends are far likelier to call a person by his or her complete name—

for example, Chen Lanfeng or Li Qiongjiu—than by the given name, Lanfeng or Qiongjiu, *sans* surname.

How one addresses another is seen in most cultures as a key indicator of the level of respect one wishes to accord, and this goes double for China, where a great deal of stock is placed in forms of address. Within families, the protocol is generally quite clear: Every blood relative has a specific title in relation to you, reflecting nature of the kinship, the relative age and even the order of birth of the person. A Chinese uncle, for example, is not just an uncle. One calls one's father's elder brother by a different title (*bobo* or *daye*) from what one calls his younger brother (*shushu*), and one's mother's brothers merit an entirely different appelation (*jiujiu*).

Within their families Chinese are traditionally called by names that indicate their order of birth; thus, the youngest male in a brood of four children is likely to be known to all as *xiaodi*, "youngest brother," and he might call his three elder sisters *dajie*, *erjie*, and *sanjie* ("eldest sister," "second elder sister," and "third elder sister"). Or the sons may be referred to as *laoda*, *lao'er*, and *laosan*, ("eldest," "second-born," "third-born") all the way to *laoyao*, which means "youngest."

While you can always call a Chinese friend by his or her name, you might also want to use a different approach if the person is a close friend. A real compliment is to call the friend by the family relationship that you *would* have had you been born into his or her family; just add the surname. So, for example, you might call a close male friend who is slightly older Chen *dage*, which means "elder brother Chen." It is considered a friendly and courteous gesture.

You have to be especially careful how you refer to your friend's relatives, however. In this area there is a bit more room for interpretation—and hence more of a danger of insult. Such forms of address are so important that they are seldom left to chance. The first time I visited the home of a friend in Taiwan, he quizzed me as to how I intended to address his father. I was surprised at the question. I had assumed it would be appropriate to use the term *xiansheng*, which can be translated as "Mister," but was quickly instructed to the contrary. To have done that would have been to have placed myself on the same generational level as his father, which would clearly *not* have been appropriate, given our relative ages. Using *xiansheng*, *taitai*, or *furen* (the latter two of which are honorific terms for "Mrs.") to address his parents would have been inappropriate also because such terms would be considered too formal.

What I learned was that you are expected to call a friend's relatives as if they were your own relatives, taking into account your relationship to the friend as well as your age and the age of your parents. The titles of choice would be *bobo* (*daye* in Beijing) and *bomu* (or possibly *shushu* and *ayi*, which are used in their place in certain regions of China), meaning "uncle" and "auntie," respectively. You should not fear appearing impertinent by such an ostensibly brazen insinuation of yourself into a friend's family structure; the Chinese take the use of these titles as compliments, and will think you very polite for knowing how to use them properly. They are part and parcel of the inclusive nature of China's social structure.

Using "uncle" and "auntie" not only shows closeness; it also establishes the generational pecking order. One reason you shouldn't call your friend's father *xiansheng* is that it would imply that you see yourself as a member of the man's generation, which would be ill bred and discourteous if you are in fact considerably younger than he is.

In business, too, it is advisable to get straight how you will address someone very early in a relationship—generally during your first meeting. For business purposes it is traditionally acceptable to call a Chinese person by the surname, together with a title such as Mister or Miss or even Minister or Managing Director. Thus Mr. Wang, Managing Director Liu, or Ms. Zhao would all be acceptable forms of address, and there's no problem with mixing an English title and a Chinese surname in just that order.

If you use Chinese, however, remember that the title *follows* the surname. So, for example, Mr. Wang would be rendered as Wang Xiansheng and Managing Director Liu would be called Liu Zongjingli, or abbreviated as Liu Zong. The more commonly used titles are listed in Figure 1.

To call someone Zhao Jingli (Manager Zhao) or the like is to use a polite form of address that has the added benefit of recognizing his or her rank and position in the balance. Interestingly, when addressing people who bear the "deputy" title—deputy managing directors, vice ministers, deputy bureau directors—you customarily omit the "deputy" or "vice" appellation and simply use *zongjingli, buzhang*, or *jüzhang*. It's more polite than specifically acknowledging the person's status as number two in the organization, though it is *not* done if the person's superior is also present. And in Beijing, a good form of address for service people—waiters, store clerks, chauffeurs, taxi drivers, and hotel employees—though not for government functionaries—is *shifu*. The term originally meant "master" (as opposed to "apprentice") and is a very refined appellation. In Shanghai and elsewhere, however, *xiansheng* and *xiaojie*—"mister" and "miss"—are more commonly used in this context.

Personal Titles

Mr.	*Xiansheng* 先生
Miss	*Xiaojie* 小姐
Ms.	*Nüshi* 女士
Madame	*Furen; Taitai* 夫人; 太太

Government Titles

President	*Zhuxi* 主席
Premier	*Zongli* 总理
Vice Premier	*Fuzongli* 副总理
Chairman	*Zhuren* 主人
Minister	*Buzhang* 部长
Bureau Director	*Jüzhang* 局长
Division Director	*Chuzhang* 处长
Governor	*Shengzhang* 省长
Mayor	*Shizhang* 市长

Corporate Titles

Chairman of the Board	*Dongshizhang* 董事长
President	*Zongcai* 总裁
Managing Director	*Zongjingli* 总经理
Manager	*Jingli* 经理
Factory Head	*Changzhang* 厂长

Figure 1. ***Commonly used titles in Chinese.*** *When speaking Chinese, the surname precedes the title. So, for example, Bureau Director Liu would be rendered as Liu Jüzhang.*

An even more gracious solution is to use the functional title and drop the surname altogether. To call Minister Li simply Buzhang, meaning "Minister," to his face is to use an extremely courteous form of address. In fact, using third person forms of address to refer to a person with whom you are talking, as in "Would the Professor like some tea?" or "Perhaps Madame Wang is too cold in this room," is especially deferential. This is as true in Taiwan and Hong Kong as it is on the mainland.

Another popular solution is to use a nickname. The endearing terms *lao* meaning "old" and *xiao* meaning "young" are quite commonly attached to surnames in China. They are said before, rather than after, the family name; thus Lao Wang (Old Wang) and Xiao Huang (Young Huang) are frequently heard. Even though they make explicit reference to age, they sometimes have as much to do with position as maturity and are not at all offensive—old age, after all, is revered in China.

And in a country where there are only a few hundred surnames in common usage—Zhang, Wang, Li, Chen, and Liu, the top five, are claimed by tens of millions of people each—there is often a need to differentiate among people in the same group. The chances of any given organization employing more than one person named Wang or Li are overwhelming; the use of these nicknames thus helps distinguish among them. Nicknames may also be cute monikers having little to do with the person's given name, like *shuaige* (good-looking brother) for a handsome young man or *xiao douzi* (little bean) for a cute child. The only caveat of which you should be aware is that these are fairly familiar forms of address, best used only when you know someone reasonably well.

In Taiwan, Hong Kong, Southeast Asia, and, indeed,

among Chinese all over the world, you can use the term *taitai* to refer to your wife, since it means "wife" as much as it does "married woman." *Xiansheng*, too, can mean "husband" in addition to "Mister." But the term *taitai* fell into disuse in the PRC after 1949, being considered too feudalistic an honorific by the communists. Their solution was the term *airen* to describe one's spouse—of either sex. *Airen* literally means "lover," and many Chinese living outside of the mainland get gooseflesh when they hear it used, since it was customarily used to describe extramarital relationships in the past. It is now slowly falling into disuse in urban China as *taitai* makes a comeback, but you will still find Chinese in some parts of the mainland who are uncomfortable using the more traditional forms.

OFFICIAL WELCOMES AND SEND-OFFS

Most travelers to China now arrive as they would in any other country. They are met at the airport by hotel representatives, tour operators, friends, company drivers, and the like. This is quite a departure from the past, when most everyone had some sort of host organization and it was the responsibility of that organization to send someone of appropriate rank to the airport to meet them.

Today, it is primarily very high-level government officials who are given formal welcomes at the airport—usually in a lounge reserved especially for this purpose. The rank of the Chinese official sent to welcome the visitors is approximately equivalent to that of the chief guest. A head of state rates another head of state or at least a vice premier; a cabinet-level official might draw a vice minister. To send anyone of significantly lesser rank would be to deliver an insult, since it would cause the visitor a loss of face.

Consider the story of a diplomat at the U.S. Embassy in Beijing who was meeting with a PRC official in charge of planning the trip to the United States of a cabinet-level minister. When the two began discussing the logistics of the visit, the American was unexpectedly lectured by his Chinese counterpart about the importance of sending an individual of sufficient stature to Dulles Airport in Washington, D.C., to greet the minister upon arrival.

The Chinese, it eventually became clear, had been seriously offended during the previous visit of a minister to the United States because the host department of the U.S. government had been able to muster only a deputy assistant secretary to do the honors at the airport. This lapse was viewed as a slight, and the official charged with planning this trip was simply trying to head off a similar unpleasant situation.

That this remains an important rite can be seen in the official send-off ceremony that is broadcast on Chinese television when senior Chinese leaders go abroad on official missions. All other senior officials line up in protocol order for a formal handshake, hockey team–style.

The same basic rules apply to seeing visitors off. The traditional polite thing to do was to escort them as far as possible. That this has become the exception rather than the rule today is probably a good indication that time is really beginning to equal money in the PRC.

Airport rituals are not absolutely necessary when you are hosting PRC guests in your own country, and they are less and less common in the business world. Indeed, in most circumstances it is not necessary to follow Chinese practices at all when interacting with Chinese in your own country. The Chinese themselves have a proverb, *Ru xiang sui su,* (Enter village, follow customs), that is the rough equivalent of the English "When in Rome, do as the Romans do." They do indeed expect things to be different abroad.

This being said, however, airport greetings are still an area where going the extra mile to follow the Chinese practice can pay off. You will score points even among well-traveled Chinese, who may appreciate the gesture even more because they know it is offered out of indulgence to them. In the case of a visit to a company headquarters by a Chinese minister, that may mean moving mountains to get the company president—or at very least a high-ranking senior vice president—to find the time to make the trek out to the airport. It might also involve mobilizing the company jet and arranging for flowers, red-carpet treatment, and limousine service. If you want to send a strong signal to a visiting Chinese dignitary, these touches can prove to be very much worth the trouble.

ON THE TELEPHONE

Doing business with the Chinese is generally accomplished through face-to-face meetings, but you are often in the position of making at least some arrangements by telephone. Making a phone call on the mainland can be an arduous process. In Taiwan and Hong Kong, where the phone systems are far more developed, getting a connection is easier and etiquette is more refined. In China, though, you may be in for an ordeal.

The telephone infrastructure in China has gotten immeasurably better in major cities over the last several years, but in the countryside it remains rudimentary, to say the least. In offices many people may share one telephone, sometimes located down the hall from where they actually do their work. Private residential phones are increasingly common, but they have not kept up with burgeoning demand, so many people still do not have their own phones at home. Sometimes they get calls on a common telephone used by their entire building or street. Increasingly, however, they solve the problem by using pagers, or even mobile phones provided by their employer.

Beware of paging services in China. I find it nearly impossible to understand the people who answer the phone at most of the services with which I have dealt in the PRC. They speak very rapidly and indistinctly, and relatively few are competent in English. However, if you remember the basic order of questions, you can negotiate the message procedure with relatively little trouble. Typically, you are first asked to give the pager number of the person you are trying to reach. The second question asks for your name, and the third question seeks your telephone number or a message. If you remember these three questions and the order in which they are asked, you can usually get your message across, even if you don't understand a word the operator is saying.

Until a few years ago it was hard even to get hold of a telephone directory in the PRC, and it's still common for people there to carry little books listing names, addresses, and phone numbers of friends and contacts. Most cities offer directory locator services, but they are more successful in finding business phone numbers than residence numbers. For this reason, you should record the phone numbers of people you hope to meet again, since it may be next to impossible to locate them by calling the main number of their organizations and asking for them by name. Switchboards are notoriously unresponsive in the PRC. I wish I had a nickel for every time I have been told someone did not exist who I knew worked at the organization or was staying in the hotel I had called. It is often advisable to persevere in such circumstances: Spell the first name, spell the last name, and if you are sure the person *should* be reachable at the number you called, keep pushing.

Chinese telephone etiquette has improved in the last several years, especially in the larger cities and in the more prestigious organizations, but still often leaves a good deal to be desired. You may be left hanging for several minutes while someone tries to find the person you are calling, for example, but don't expect to be kept apprised of what is going on.

The standard greeting you get when a phone is answered is the word *wei*, which means "hello" and which, like its English counterpart, is basically an attention-getter. The word *wei* may shift in meaning, however, depending upon how it is used in the conversation. At the beginning, *wei* means nothing more than "I'm on; now it's your turn to talk." When the conversation does begin it's a good idea to verify that you have reached the organization you intended to dial, since Chinese often do not furnish any identifying information upon answering the phone. *Wei* may also be used at times, in the middle of a sentence, to mean "Are you still there?" or "Keep quiet for a moment, I'm about to say something important."

There is a certain suspicion that pervades telephone calls in the PRC, perhaps a lingering legacy of the Cultural Revolution, and unless you are known or immediately identifiable to the person who answers, you are likely to get little information until you have told a good deal of your own story. That includes for whom you work and why you are calling as well as the person with whom you wish to speak. If you fail to provide these specifics, you may be questioned about them. Typically you will be asked *Ni naiwei?* meaning, literally, "Who are you?" or *Ni nali?* or *Ni nar?* meaning "Where are you?"

Neither of these questions should be taken at face value; both are ways of asking the same thing, which is really "What organization do you represent?" A Chinese at work likely cares little about your individual identity, still less where you happen to be located when making the call. He or she is trying to establish through this line of questioning what your organization is, and what issue you are calling about. That's all that really matters. So as much of an assault as it may be on your sense of self, the proper way to identify yourself on the phone in China is by naming your organization: "I am IBM" or "I am the Royal Dutch Embassy" are the types of responses that are expected.

Your impulse at this point may be to try to brush off the excessively curious person who has answered the phone and insist on talking with the individual you are calling. Sometimes this works, but often you have to go through a certain amount of interrogation before the person calls your party to the phone. It's common to provide a capsule summary of what has led up to the call, and many people refuse to settle for less.

Part of the problem is that even senior officials don't have secretaries in the Western sense of the word. While many do have a subordinate they refer to as their *mishu* (secretary), this is not a clerical position but rather a high level aide-de-camp. So anyone who answers a phone call feels it incumbent on him- or herself to understand the entire matter at hand in case he or she is asked later on.

Once all is made clear, and the person on the other end of the line is satisfied that he or she has gleaned all of the information needed from you, either you will be connected with the person you are seeking or you'll get an answer about the meeting. Although you may wish to hear confirmation directly from your contact person, this is not really necessary; in China, people speak for their work units, and they generally don't speak at all if they aren't sure where the unit stands. So if someone presumes to tell you that a meeting has been okayed, it usually has.

If the person you are seeking is out, leave a message at your own risk. Secretaries are not yet commonplace, and office mates often discourage you from leaving word, suggesting that you call back later. This absolves them of any responsibility for taking and transmitting the message. If they are willing to take your name and number, there is still a chance the party will never find out that you called, or at least not find out until he or she happens to return to the office, or happens to ask if anyone called. In essence, they do not see ensuring that the message is received as part of their responsibility, and so they will often not go out of their way to deliver it.

Generally speaking, while it is increasingly possible to conduct business on the telephone in China, for reasons that have as much to do with technology as culture, it is probably still best transacted in person.

Recap: Eight Reminders on Meeting and Greeting

1. Names are very important to the Chinese, and you must establish how to address someone during your first meeting. Chinese are seldom called by their given names, except by close relatives or extremely intimate friends.
2. Chinese surnames come first, not last. Call a Chinese person by the surname, together with a title such as Mister or Miss or even Director or Manager. You may also drop the surname altogether and call the person by the functional title only.
3. While you can always call a Chinese friend by his or her name, you might also want to call the friend by the family relationship that you would have had you been born into his or her family, such as *dage* for an elder male or *xiaomei* for a younger female. This goes for the friend's relatives as well. For his or her parents, use "uncle" and "auntie."
4. For an especially gracious form of business address, drop the "deputy" in any official's title, and you may also drop the surname altogether. To call Vice Minister Li simply Buzhang, meaning "Minister," to his face is to use an extremely courteous form of address.
5. Formal welcoming parties are sent to airports by the Chinese to meet important delegations and see them off, but this is now seen more in the diplomatic world than the business world. The rank of the official greeter depends on the importance of the visitors.
6. When you host Chinese abroad, it is not absolutely necessary to meet or see delegations off at the airport unless the group is high-ranking. However, airport rituals are

highly appreciated, and you will score points even among well-traveled Chinese if you make the effort.

7. In dealing with Chinese paging services, remember the order of questions: the number being paged, your name, and your phone number. This helps you deal with switchboard operators who speak rapidly and indistinctly.
8. Resign yourself to the fact that you may have to give more information to a person who answers the phone than you wish if you want that person to give you any help—including leaving a message or connecting you to the party you are calling.

Chapter IV

Some Basic Cultural Differences

INDIVIDUALISM VERSUS GROUP-CENTEREDNESS

THE SINGLE MOST IMPORTANT AND FUNDAMENTAL DIFFERence between Chinese and Westerners is undoubtedly the role played by the individual in the society. In the West, we place a strong emphasis on personal achievement, creativity, and initiative. We glory in our individual differences, nurture them and value them as the essential features that make us unique. Indeed, uniqueness is a goal unto itself in America; it's vitally important to us that we *not* be exactly like other people.

Who in the West hasn't been admonished to be your own person, or to look out for yourself because no one else can be counted on to look out for you? Who has never been praised for standing up for your personal beliefs, especially when the tide of opinion is flowing in the opposite direction? The premium among Western peoples is not on conformity; it is on individual expression and rugged independence.

In China, on the other hand—and on both sides of the Taiwan Strait—children are given an entirely different set of messages: Don't question the world around you or try to change it; accept it. Submit willingly and unquestioningly to authority. Your importance as an individual is not nearly as great as that of the role you play in a larger group.

In Imperial China, that larger group would have been one's extended family—grandparents, father, mother, siblings, uncles, aunts, and cousins of all descriptions, all of whom might well have lived together in the same family compound. In modern-day China it might be one's nuclear family, one's class at school, one's military unit, fellow members of a delegation, or one's *danwei* (work unit—see below), depending on one's time of life. The situation varies; the dynamics, however, are much the same no matter what the group is.

Group process in China is not based merely on the authority of the leaders; a real premium is placed on consensus. Matters are often debated at great length until agreement is reached on a course of action. Once a decision has been made, however, individual group members are expected to fall in line, embrace it, and act on it, and nobody presumes to question it, at least overtly.

This is one reason that a dozen years ago you seldom heard a Chinese make an irreverent comment, or openly express a view at odds with that of his or her unit. Toeing the line is important, and it was enforced when party discipline was a stronger force with which to be reckoned. In the post-Tiananmen era, however, people are far more likely to express their true views, provided the situation is right and they do not feel threatened.

In essence, Chinese enter into a sort of compact with their groups; in exchange for obedience and loyalty, they can expect protection and support, and be confident that their well-being will be a matter of concern to the group as a whole. Group membership requires discipline: You must subordinate your own will to that of the whole, and make decisions based not on personal selfishness, but on the best interests of the larger group. Chinese people must listen to those in authority and do as they say. And their actions, for good or ill, reflect not only on themselves but also on all of their compatriots.

For example, take the case of Chinese tennis star Hu Na, who defected to the United States from the PRC in the early 1980s. The American government, in reaching the decision to grant her political asylum, cited, among other things, the fact that Ms. Hu did not wish to return to the PRC. But the Chinese position was that the young woman's wishes were only one consideration, and a minor one at that. It was also important to take into account the interests and desires of her parents, her work unit, and the government of the society that had given her so much, all of which were ostensibly aligned in wishing for her speedy return to China.

The discussion of telephone etiquette in Chapter 3 provides still another illustration of the preeminence of the group in Chinese society. You'll recall that traditionally you did not not need to identify yourself personally when answering the telephone; what was deemed important was your work unit. The fact that it is still common practice to answer "I am the Ministry of Finance" rather than "I am Guo Yang" speaks volumes about the relative importance of the individual and the group.

So does the fact that it is units, and not individuals, that invite foreign guests, arrange activities for them, and sign contracts with them. None of this should be interpreted to mean that the Chinese do not possess unique personalities, however. They most certainly do. The distinction lies in the issue of when and under what circumstances it is permissible for people to express their individual differences.

Although Chinese people must be ever vigilant in fulfilling obligations to fellow group members, it's important to note that as a rule they feel no comparable responsibility toward outsiders other than guests. Courtesy and hospitality are frequently not forthcoming when Chinese deal with people with whom they have no connections. Indeed, they are capable of treating one another with indifference that can border on cruelty. The us-them dichotomy often surfaces in the work of the government in the form of intractable bureaucratic rivalries that impede progress and innovation.

It has sometimes been pointed out that one of Chinese culture's major failings is that its people just don't know how to treat outsiders. Ironically but fortunately, foreigners have typically been exempt from this kind of treatment, their very foreignness earning them favorable treatment as honored guests. Whether this will continue into the future when foreigners become even more like fixtures on the landscape than honored guests remains to be seen.

THE *DANWEI*—THE WORK UNIT

Under orthodox communism, it was the work unit, or *danwei*, that wielded the most power over an individual's life in mainland China. Employers in Taiwan and Hong Kong probably hold more sway over the lives of their employees than those in the West, but they never had anywhere near as much influence as the *danwei* in the PRC did. On the mainland, the work unit had a say in just about all major decisions in a worker's life, and in a great number of minor ones as well.

Traditionally, Chinese did not choose their work units; they were assigned to them after they finished their education through a system that was as inefficient as it was impersonal, since individual preferences were largely irrelevant to the process. To compound the problem, there was typically almost no job mobility in the PRC. Someone assigned to be a factory worker, for example, could for all practical purposes expect to work in the same factory for the rest of his or her working life, though promotions and job changes within the unit were possible, especially for Party members. Switching to another *danwei* was difficult if not impossible, the principal route being job swapping, accomplished through *guanxi* (see below) or, later, through advertising.

The influence of a typical Chinese unit extended far beyond employees' working lives and well into their personal lives. Not only did the unit decide what job you did, how much you were paid, and when promotions came; it also controlled where you lived, how much living space you were allocated, when you could marry, and whether and when you could travel or study abroad. Through your work unit—and *only* through your work unit—you could obtain coupons that permitted you to purchase certain scarce commodities. At various times in the last fifty years pork, sugar, eggs, salt, grain, cooking oil, cotton cloth, gas, coal, bicycles, and wooden furniture were all rationed in the PRC. The unit also controlled access to health care and child care, paid pensions to retired workers, and enforced the government's one-child policy.

This *danwei* system, which was set up by the communists in the 1950s, remains today, though in a decided state of decline. As foreign institutions like representative offices, joint ventures, and wholly owned foreign enterprises have become employers, and as government bureaucracies have been supplanted by progressive state-owned enterprises and collective or private employers, the tyranny of the *danwei* has become more and more a thing of the past.

One of the functions retained by the *danwei* today is to keep custody of an individual's *dang'an* (file). The file is a record of the individual's life, work, and behavior, and it is necessary for certain functions, especially when the individual wants to apply for a passport or switch employers, or if he or she gets into trouble with the authorities. Sometimes possession of a person's *dang'an* can be used by the *danwei* for leverage, and there are many examples of universities holding students' files for ransom when the students get jobs in the private sector: The *danwei* insists on being paid a fee to release the file, ostensibly to offset the cost of the tuition paid by the government to educate a worker who now will not be serving the state after all. I know a Chinese who actually asked his *danwei* to fire him outright so he would not have to pay a "ransom" for his *dang'an*.

Despite this, the control of the *danwei* diminishes with each passing year. Today there is a great deal of mobility; jobs are advertised and filled by applicants in a more or less supply-and-demand fashion. Parents accustomed to the old system sit in wonderment at the frequent job changes of their children. Employers now retain the right to hire and fire. Subsidies to government employees have been reduced to bare bones and are generally limited to housing, medical care (which is less and less subsidized), and unemployment compensation. And there are far fewer intrusions into individuals' personal affairs. As enterprises—both foreign and Chinese-owned—grow in importance, the control exerted by the *danwei* is quite likely to diminish even further. As far as most Chinese are concerned, it is a case of good riddance.

Confucianism

The position of the individual in Chinese society cannot be fully understood without a discussion of the thought of the sage Confucius (551–479 B.C.) and his disciples, which has exerted a potent influence on Chinese culture through the centuries. Confucianism is actually more a system of ethics and morals than a religion per se, and it stresses the obligations of people to one another as a function of the relationships among them.

It would be hard to overstate the contribution of Confucius, who delineated the responsibilities of individuals toward one another based on five important human relationships—those between ruler and subject, husband and wife, father and son, brother and brother, and friend and friend. He advocated a social order that emphasized duty, loyalty, honor, filial piety, respect for age and seniority, and sincerity. Such traits remain valued among Chinese the world over even to this day, surviving even a brief period toward the end of the Cultural Revolution when Confucius' teachings were severely criticized on the mainland as feudalistic and counterrevolutionary.

Confucius' philosophy can be seen at work in myriad ways

in China today. Deference to people in authority and to elders is an obvious one. Chinese are seldom guilty of overt insubordination, and are taught to know their place in any given hierarchy and the attendant responsibilities this implies. Characteristic Chinese unwillingness to depart from the straight and narrow path set by the leaders is also traceable to Confucius; to do otherwise would mean to fail in one's duty and to be disloyal.

China's bureaucracy probably owes as much to its Confucian heritage as it does to the Soviet Union, on whose government structure it was largely modeled. Far from the "classless" organization of communist mythology, it is in fact strictly hierarchical, with rank and its privileges defined extremely clearly. People relate to one another not purely as individuals, but rather according to their relative ranks. Decision-making is strictly top-down, and nothing much is accomplished without support from the higher echelons. Personal loyalty is highly valued, and it is common for high-ranking cadres to install cronies in important positions under their control.

Confucianism is an inherently conservative belief system. It suffers innovation badly, and does nothing whatever to encourage it. On the contrary; a hierarchical, vertical system of government in which decisions of even minor import must be referred upward is no crucible for revolutionary change. No one is willing to stick his or her neck out, and so new ground is seldom broken, except by those at the very top. Characteristically, the Chinese bureaucracy is notorious for long delays and nearly imperceptible progress.

In Confucius' ideal society, each individual occupies his or her proper place—rank is critical, and there is no real equality. In his writings, Confucius spoke frequently of the "superior man," who embodies a number of virtues, most of which are as highly valued among Chinese today as they have ever been. Traditionally, there are eight such virtues: *zhong* (loyalty), *xiao* (filial piety), *ren* (benevolence), *ai* (love), *xin* (trust), *yi* (justice), *he* (harmony), and *ping* (peace). The superior man embodies all of these in some measure.

The superior man is modest, even self-deprecating; he is moderate in habits, generous, and given to compromise and conciliation rather than direct confrontation. He has no need to parade his belongings or his accomplishments before others. He is driven by a well-developed sense of duty. He endeavors to make others comfortable and is solicitous of guests. He never loses his balance or his temper, and remains poised no matter what the situation. A man of integrity, he overlooks deficiencies in others and demonstrates honesty and propriety in all of his dealings.

Confucius and all he stood for took a major drubbing in China during the tumultuous Cultural Revolution period from the mid 1960s to the mid 1970s, when his teachings were widely and vehemently criticized as bourgeois and counterrevolutionary. But since that time there has been a pronounced return to Confucian values. The government has manufactured several propaganda campaigns since the early 1980s, urging people to return to civilized behavior, which to the Chinese really means Confucian mores.

Mianzi—Face

Another important cultural concept is that of *mianzi*, which is Chinese for "face." The Chinese are acutely sensitive to the regard in which they are held by others or the light in which they appear, and it is very important to be aware of the concept of *mianzi* if only to head off situations in which you cause someone to lose it. The consequences can be severe. At the very least you will cease to receive cooperation from the person; you are quite likely as well to open yourself up to some form of retaliation.

Face is a fragile commodity in China, and there are many ways in which one can cause someone else to lose it. One sure way is to dress down a person or insult him or her in front of peers. Another is to treat someone as if his or her feelings do not matter, or to be deliberately patronizing. Failing to treat someone with proper respect is a real sin among the Chinese, and it almost always comes back to haunt you. For if you cause someone to lose face you will not only lose the respect of the person you have wronged; you will also lose that of others who are aware of your transgression. A detailed discussion of face and its implications can be found in Chapter 11.

The story in the last chapter of the Chinese minister who was insulted after being met at the airport by a deputy assistant secretary is an excellent case study in *mianzi*. The reason the Chinese were so furious at the treatment the minister received was that it appeared to them that the U.S. government was delivering a deliberate slap in the face. Only after it was made clear that the offense had been inadvertent rather than deliberate could the Chinese forgive; forgetting was always out of the question.

I can offer another, more personal story about losing face. I once wrote a letter to a Chinese minister in an attempt to set up a meeting with him for my boss, who was coming to China the following month. In the letter I mentioned that he would be visiting China at the personal invitation of a vice premier.

In point of fact, although the vice premier had indeed suggested to my boss that he lead a delegation to China, the actual invitation had been issued by our host organization, which interpreted my comments as patronizing.

I was summoned the very next day by the host unit and summarily dressed down for my perceived offense. I explained that I had certainly not intended a slight, and to this day believe that my hosts overreacted to the situation. But offense exists in the eye of the beholder, and my intentions were seen as somewhat less important than my crime. The matter was not ended to their satisfaction until I wrote a formal retraction, which of course was a blow to my own prestige. The fact that I was caused to lose face in the process was of little concern because I was seen as responsible for the whole situation. Having delivered the first blow, I apparently had no right to expect any magnanimity in my host unit's posture toward me. And, indeed, I got none.

The vehemence of the unit's reaction surprised me, but it really just underscores how important face is to the Chinese. When you cause someone to lose it, you can just about count on retribution of one type or another. The Chinese do not often show anger; to do so would fly in the face of the Confucian virtues. They do, however, get even. And while active confrontation would be viewed as unacceptable behavior on the part of the superior man, passive aggression is always fair. The Chinese, in fact, are masters of the art. It can take different forms, but often appears as "inability" to accomplish something they know you wish to get done, or failure to show up at an appointed time with an obviously fabricated excuse. At no point, however, is etiquette likely to be breached.

The concept of face certainly exists in the West as well, but not to the same degree as it does in the East. In the West people tend to be more willing to forgive slights that cause them to lose face. Friendly hazing is, after all, somewhat acceptable in the Western world. Name-calling, playful dressing down, and sarcastic commentary may occur, but all is seen as good, clean fun. Such behavior, however, seldom occurs among Asians, for whom face is always very serious business.

In English you can lose face and you can save face; in Chinese, however, you can also *give* face. Giving face means doing something to enhance someone else's reputation or prestige. Complimenting a worker to his or her superior and publicly recognizing someone's efforts are good ways of giving face. Thanking someone who has worked hard on a particular project, even someone of very low rank, is also an excellent example of this. Such actions carry a great deal of weight among Chinese when they come from foreign guests.

My host organization once placed me in the seat of honor next to its chairman during a reception held in Beijing. Though I was flattered by the attention, I did not think much of it until a representative of that organization approached me for a favor a few months later. To ensure my compliance, he was careful to remind me of how much face the unit had accorded me through that action.

One of my favorite examples of giving face is a volleyball game in which I once participated at the Chinese Embassy in Washington. The embassy team played volleyball nearly every day; it was their chief form of recreation and exercise. The American challengers, on the other hand, were a pickup team that had never really practiced together and whose members varied tremendously in skill. From the beginning it was clear that this was not to be a serious match; it had been billed as more of a social occasion than anything else. But from the start the Chinese played to win, and win they did. The first game was, as I recall, a shutout.

The second game turned out to be quite the opposite. Without so much as a word being spoken among them, the Chinese team members suddenly started to miss shots they had had no trouble making during the previous game. In the end they tallied up a respectable score, but it was the Americans who won—or, as I quickly realized, had been *permitted* to win—the second game. Had it been a legitimate test of skill, the Chinese would no doubt have played mercilessly, and the second game would have ended up very much like the first. But it was a social gathering, and it would have been unsociable to cause guests to lose self-respect—face—in such a situation. Far better to even out the score and let everyone go away feeling like a winner.

GUANXI—CONNECTIONS

It's often the case that you can't even get to first base in China without *guanxi*, and you can do just about anything—even things you probably ought *not* to do—when you have it. *Guanxi* really means "connections." It has everything to do with whom you know and what these people are willing—or obligated—to do for you.

To the Chinese, *guanxi* is a sort of tit-for-tat, "You scratch my back, I'll scratch yours" arrangement. Someone with whom you have *guanxi* can be counted on to do you favors, bend the rules, and even break them sometimes on your behalf. It is a cultural phenomenon common to Chinese all over the world, and by no means the exclusive province of the PRC. In China, however—which has had until recently an economy of scarcity—*guanxi* has proven particularly useful in gaining access to goods and services otherwise difficult or impossible to come by, or in getting inside information.

Guanxi is, of course, a reciprocal obligation. You are expected to behave in similar fashion and to deliver favors to those with whom you have *guanxi*. Nor need the currency of *guanxi* be cash—it seldom is, in fact. You might be asked to procure hard-to-get theater tickets, arrange an appointment with a well-known doctor, introduce someone to a potential business partner, secure a visa for someone, or recommend someone for a trip abroad.

Guanxi often involves going in via the *houmen* (back door), which is discussed in more detail in Chapter 12. Going through the back door is often the only effective way to get certain things accomplished in the PRC.

The Chinese generally expect foreigners to understand *guanxi* and behave according to its rules. A woman I knew in Beijing once explained to me that she had worked hard to develop *guanxi* within her work unit in order to establish a relationship with someone who had access to the chop—the official seal—of the unit. This person could be counted on to stamp her application to the Public Security Bureau for a passport. In turn, a former colleague of her father's who was well placed at the Bureau could probably be counted on to ensure that the application would be approved after it was submitted, and that a passport would be issued.

She lacked only *guanxi* at the U.S. Embassy, which would of course have to issue her a visa before she could travel to the United States—her fondest wish. That was where I was to come in; although she knew I was not a diplomat, she figured that as an American I was very likely to know someone at the embassy whom I could pressure on her behalf. When I attempted to explain to her that the U.S. system didn't quite work the same way and that I had no particular sway with the U.S. consular officers, who in any event were required to follow the rules in issuing visas, it was like talking to a brick wall. I had a dreadfully difficult time convincing her that I wasn't simply shirking what she perceived as my responsibility as her friend and refusing to help.

This same woman once asked a colleague of mine who was leaving for a trip to Hong Kong to buy something for her that was not available on the mainland. My associate generously agreed to bring it back for her. It turned out, however, that the item wasn't even intended for her—it was really for a friend of hers. She was using her *guanxi* with my colleague to do a favor for a friend to whom she herself had an obligation. When the deed was done, my co-worker and I were invited to a dinner hosted by the recipient as a way of expressing her appreciation. But since her parents' apartment was too small to accommodate all the people, the home of another friend was borrowed for the purpose. Again, *guanxi* at work.

Reciprocity

Closely related to the concept of *guanxi* is that of reciprocity. Many Chinese look at relationships at least partially through a "What's-in-it-for-me" lens, and friendships are not necessarily sought exclusively for reasons of personal enjoyment. Reciprocity is as much a factor in interpersonal relationships as it is in business dealings, and what it means, ultimately, is that the economy of favors between two individuals or units is expected to remain in rough balance over a period of time. Reciprocity is the reason Chinese people feel comfortable presuming on those with whom they have *guanxi*; if they have done a favor for a friend, they feel they are owed a favor in return.

One corollary to this rule is that Chinese will not only gladly grant favors to friends who request them, they will sometimes do favors that are not requested, with the idea that they can use them to justify payback sometime in the future. A Westerner I know engaged a Chinese teacher to tutor his teenage son in music, and did not think much of it when the teacher began to bring his own son along when he came to the foreigner's home to teach. The boys were about the same age, and the Chinese youth often brought small gifts along. The teacher even began to shorten the lessons to give the boys enough time to play together. After a few months had passed, the teacher approached the foreign father and asked for his help finding a job with a foreign company for his son, who would soon graduate. He obviously felt that in light of the friendship between the boys and the gifts that had changed hands, his son had racked up something of a chit that could be called in.

A second corollary to this rule is that you should proceed with caution before putting a Chinese in a position in which he or she is totally unable to return a favor. Giving an extremely expensive gift can place the recipient in an uncomfortable situation. If there is no possibility of the person's ever repaying the gift with something of approximately equal value, he or she will always be beholden to the giver—or else lose face.

Sometimes someone seeking a favor will approach even a relative stranger with a gift. Though it is seldom stated overtly, the obvious implication is that accepting the gift means accepting an obligation to perform the favor. If you do not wish to be beholden to such a supplicant, you should decline the present (see Chapter 9).

The Chinese New Year—called Spring Festival on the mainland—is a common time chosen to settle accounts, and many gifts change hands at this time of the year. People visit friends, colleagues, bosses, and business associates bearing fruit, preserved meats, and other presents that may be very expensive. Sometimes they are repaying specific favors done for them in the course of the previous year; other times it is more like positioning themselves for favors they may need to ask in the future.

It's worth noting that Chinese are exceptionally diligent about keeping track of the value of gifts received or given; at weddings, for example, the amount of a cash gift is dutifully recorded at a sign-in table before one sits down to eat. This permits the recipient to reciprocate accordingly when the opportunity arises. An expensive New Year's gift might be in order, for example, if an expensive gift was received at your daughter's wedding earlier in the year.

Guanxi is not necessarily an inexhaustible commodity. A former colleague of mine once treated his organization's relationship with a Chinese official as if it were, and the strategy backfired badly. Because his company had once hosted a delegation led by this official in the United States, my friend constantly asked this person for favors. He was successful up to a point—the point, presumably, at which the Chinese official figured that the obligation had pretty much been repaid. After that, when the requests did not cease, the Chinese official became more remote and less available. The relationship ultimately deteriorated until my friend's telephone calls to the unit were no longer returned.

Privacy

I count views of privacy as a basic cultural difference not because the Chinese would consider it a particularly important concept in their society, but because Westerners find it to be conspicuous in its absence. There is no direct translation in Chinese for the English word "privacy"; the notion simply doesn't exist in the same way among most Chinese people.

Perhaps the difference comes from the fact that the idea of being alone and unobserved has never had much meaning in a land that has always been overpopulated and overcrowded, where a half dozen people may live in one room, and where there has never been much mobility. Chinese children do not, by and large, grow up with their own rooms at home; doors are open within the home, and all members of the family have access to all rooms at will, no matter who sleeps where. There is little notion of private space within the family group.

Prying eyes are everywhere on the mainland, aimed not only in the direction of foreigners, but also at the Chinese themselves. People generally have few secrets from fellow employees in their *danwei,* who in the past were encouraged to report suspicious activities. Even neighbors—though less so now than in the past—know one another's business, and people are very much aware of the comings and goings of those around them.

This can be seen as a form of social control, and indeed it is; suspicious goings-on are noted and sometimes reported to the authorities. One of the many unfortunate consequences of the Cultural Revolution, during which people were encouraged to inform on one another if any bourgeois activities were suspected, is that many people in China harbor suspicion of other Chinese they do not know well. Only close friends may be completely trusted.

Even in apartments or hotels, where foreigners expect to find privacy, they are often foiled. In Chinese-style hotels, service personnel are everywhere, and they are easily able to keep tabs on who comes in, with whom, and when. Hotel staff sometimes enter guest rooms at will, often without knocking first. This is not a problem in the joint venture hotels, but there are still security personnel on hand wherever foreigners live. Their job is supposedly to prevent theft and keep out those who have no legitimate business in foreign-resident compounds, but the general consensus among most foreigners is that security guards are also there to keep an eye on them and their activities, and to report any suspicious goings-on.

Given the lack of private space, when the Chinese need to be alone, they often go outside for a walk. There is enough anonymity in the larger cities, especially after dusk, to allow people to be apart with their own thoughts. Where the real problem comes in is when couples wish some privacy for courting or love-making. So few single people have access to private quarters that if they can't persuade a roommate to make him- or herself scarce for a period of time, they, too, will take to the streets. Public parks in nearly any large city in

China are jammed after dark with young couples locked in passionate embrace who literally have nowhere else to go. It is ironic that only in the most public of situations can many Chinese find privacy.

Finally, there is also an entirely different aspect of privacy that is basic to the Chinese; it is the privacy of one's own thoughts and feelings. Keeping one's emotions to oneself is not only a Chinese custom; it is considered a highly desirable attainment. The impassive expression Westerners observe when they look into the faces of many of their Chinese friends, which no doubt gave rise to the common use of the adjective "inscrutable" in describing Chinese people, is something that is, in fact, socialized into Chinese children from birth.

Not surprisingly, Chinese report being able to read emotions on Western faces—many of which are really an open book—as a novel experience. Many find it a refreshing change of pace to be able to deduce feelings so easily from facial expressions. It also provides a definite advantage to the Chinese when they participate in negotiations with foreigners.

RECAP: ELEVEN POINTS ON CULTURAL DIFFERENCES

1. Chinese are socialized not to question the social order or try to change it. They submit willingly and relatively unquestioningly to authority, and learn that group membership is more important than individuality. The actions of individuals reflect not only on themselves, but on all of their compatriots in a group.
2. The Chinese place a real premium on consensus. Matters are debated until agreement is reached on a course

of action. When this happens, the decision of the leader is the final word. Individual group members are expected to embrace and act on it regardless of their personal views.

3. The *danwei* (work unit) traditionally wielded tremendous power over the lives of individuals in China, controlling where one worked, where one lived, and where one could travel as well as one's ration of scarce commodities. This system is in an advanced state of decay, but the *danwei* can still be a potent force controlling individuals' lives in certain situations.
4. The Confucian system of ethics and morals governs much of the way Chinese interact with one another even today. It emphasizes duty, loyalty, filial piety, sincerity, and respect for age and seniority. Deference to authority and to elders, rank-consciousness, modesty, moderation in habits, generosity, and avoidance of direct confrontation are all highly valued Confucian traits.
5. Confucianism also helps explain China's bureaucracy—strictly hierarchical, with well-defined ranks and privileges. Decision-making is strictly top-down, personal loyalty is highly valued, cronyism is rampant and innovation largely stifled.
6. Face, or *mianzi*—the regard in which one is held by others or the light in which one appears—is vitally important to the Chinese. Causing someone to lose face, through a public insult or dressing-down, or by failing to treat him or her with respect, results in a loss of cooperation and often in retaliation. If you do so you will also lose the respect of others aware of your transgression.

7. In China, face cannot only be lost and saved, it can also be given. Doing something to enhance someone's reputation or prestige, such as lauding a worker to his or her superior, is an example. Such actions carry a great deal of weight among Chinese when they come from foreigners.
8. *Guanxi* (connections) is a tit-for-tat arrangement between people or work units that makes the Chinese system go. It offers you access to goods and services otherwise difficult to acquire. The currency of *guanxi* is normally favors, not cash. Chinese generally expect foreigners to understand *guanxi* and behave according to its rules.
9. The balance sheet between two individuals or units is expected to remain in rough balance over a period of time. Beware of unsolicited favors, as they usually have a price. Try not to put a Chinese in the position of being unable to return a favor, and don't accept presents or favors unless you are prepared to reciprocate.
10. Prying eyes are everywhere in China; local Chinese are watched, as are foreigners. In foreigners' apartments and some hotels, service personnel keep tabs on the guests. Suspicious goings-on are reported.
11. Unlike Westerners, who may be open books, Chinese are socialized from birth to keep their feelings from showing on their faces. This is why they are sometimes described as "inscrutable."

Chapter V

Lijie: The Fine Art of Politeness

IT DOESN'T REALLY MATTER MUCH WHETHER YOU ADMIRE someone a great deal or wish him or her in the depths of hell. In China, your personal feelings toward others have precious little to do with how you deal with them publicly. To be Chinese is to know instinctively how to treat another person so as to appear impeccably gracious, but perhaps even more important, so as to avoid even the hint of criticism.

What the Chinese call *lijie* translates as "etiquette," "manners," or "courtesy," and it is really much more a matter of form than of substance. A Westerner might ask a guest if he or she wishes a drink, and even detail a list of available beverages, but if the guest declines, nothing is served. Not so for a Chinese host, for whom this would constitute an inexcusable breach of manners. In a Chinese home, an obligatory glass of tea is immediately set out in front of every arriving guest, no questions asked. Even the strongest protest is essentially ignored. And the fact that the tea may never even be tasted in no way negates the propriety of the gesture.

While the ostensible purpose of Chinese courtesy is to make a guest comfortable, the emphasis, ultimately, is more on doing the correct and proper thing. "To the Westerner," wrote Dr. Arthur H. Smith in 1894 in his book *Chinese Characteristics*, "politeness is 'real kindness kindly expressed.' To the Chinese it is no such thing . . . it is a ritual of technicalities." How well one follows those rituals and attends to the technicalities translates into how well schooled in *lijie* one is. And in China, no one is criticized for being *too* polite; if anything, one is complimented for it!

Surface Harmony

The key to understanding Chinese courtesy is to grasp the central importance of surface harmony, the god to which just about everything is sacrificed in China. Regardless of one's true feelings, regardless of what is really going on under the surface, one is always expected to behave with decorum, and never to do anything to cause a moment of public unpleasantness or embarrassment. Such behavior is one of the hallmarks of what Confucius referred to as the "superior man."

As with matters pertaining to face, the world of Chinese etiquette has little use for truth in the sense of expressing genuine feelings if these are not pleasant. Few Chinese would see much value, for example, in reproving a colleague for doing something that made them angry or upset, even though to a Westerner clearing the air in this way would generally be seen as something very positive, for it might prevent the same thing from happening again. To a Chinese, the premium is on doing things more for show than for substance. Regardless of the actual circumstances, those truly proficient in Chinese manners set their sights on maintaining superficial pleasantness at all times.

This dynamic is partially responsible for a phenomenon many Westerners have observed about their Chinese colleagues: their propensity, at times, to remain very quiet even in meetings characterized by a lot of give-and-take among the other participants. A Chinese person who does not agree with a point of view being expressed or a plan that is being announced by a new boss will not necessarily speak out against it, for to do so would disturb the surface harmony. Better to remain quiet and "give face" to the boss than to openly defy him or her in public. Foreigners are thus well advised not to mistake silence for assent in China.

The Chinese, of course, do not lack ways of communicating criticism, disdain, disgust, or resentment, and they are not incapable of sabotage, subversion, or revenge. They simply do it with more subtlety than their Western counterparts. It would be a faux pas of the worst order to make such negative feelings manifest through overt behavior. Passive resistance can be every bit as effective as the active kind, and it goes the active kind one better in that it is hard to detect, and need not involve any disturbance in the surface harmony.

USING INTERMEDIARIES

The unavoidable need to preserve both surface harmony and face at all times is largely responsible for the Chinese penchant for using intermediaries to carry unpleasant news. Because there is not only no premium on confrontation, but also no excuse for it, Chinese prefer whenever possible to communicate unpleasant truths or complaints quietly through third parties. They also use intermediaries to make inquiries that are best not made directly. The only exception to this rule is when unpleasantness or anger may be expressed directly for the strategic purpose of extracting concessions or otherwise putting the opposite number in a defensive posture during negotiations or other stressful situations.

Not long ago, a colleague of mine approached me because she knew that the foreign boss in the company in which her cousin worked was a good friend of mine. That company had just moved to a new office, and her cousin had been assigned to a desk in a remote corner of the suite, far from his colleagues. The neighboring desks were vacant, and he was perplexed at the treatment he was getting. What did it all mean? Why was he sitting all by himself? Was he well regarded in the company? Could he expect a promotion at some point? Rather than approach his boss directly with these questions and risk a potentially face-losing scenario, he asked my colleague to ask me to ask his foreign boss what the story was. Why risk being direct when you can get information indirectly?

Consider the plight of a foreign friend of mine who was dating a Chinese woman, but who was increasingly dissatisfied at her seeming indifference to him. In true foreign fashion, he pressed the issue with her several times, demanding to know where he stood. He never really got a straight answer about what was going on, however. Not, that is, until her best friend engineered a tête-à-tête with him. She used this highly contrived opportunity—no doubt carefully scripted and rehearsed—to break the news that the girlfriend was in fact still in love with her previous beau and didn't think he would ever measure up to this predecessor.

In a Western context, this was surely information that ought to have come to him directly from his girlfriend, and he was confused and hurt that he had to learn this painful truth from her friend rather than from her. But what might appear an act of cowardice to a Westerner could in fact be viewed by a Chinese as an act of kindness. To her way of thinking, in sparing him the direct humiliation of being told by his lover that she preferred another, she was also sparing his face. (For a fuller discussion of face, see Chapter 11.) And she was averting confrontation that in the Chinese view would be as wholly unnecessary as it would be unpleasant. Why cause a scene when the same information could be communicated equally clearly, but far more humanely, by remote control?

Never mind the fact that communicating in this indirect way precludes the give-and-take that most Westerners would require in order to gain clarity and reach resolution in such a situation. While explicitness and some sort of accountability would matter a great deal to a foreigner, to a Chinese the preservation of face and surface harmony would trump them every time.

Intermediaries play at least as important a role in business as they do in matters of the heart. They are highly useful in negotiations, for example, for floating trial balloons that do not ever have to be acknowledged if they prove to be unacceptable. They provide back channels for information that might prove too sensitive or risky to transmit through formal channels. They help companies make requests of others that run the risk of being turned down. And they communicate unpleasant information that Chinese people generally find much easier to receive from others than from its true source.

THE CHINESE CIRCLE

One way of looking at how Chinese people manage their social relationships is to think in terms of an imaginary circle that surrounds every Chinese person. People fall into one of two categories: inside or outside the circle. Those inside the circle are relatives, who come first, and then friends, neighbors, classmates, and co-workers as well as pretty much anyone who has been introduced by someone belonging to one of these groups. That is, those inside the circle are those with whom one has some form of *guanxi* (see Chapter 10) and hence to whom one bears some sort of obligation.

The rest of the world remains outside of the circle. These are the people a Chinese person does not know, and to whom he or she has no particular obligation. They are those one brushes up against on the street without a word of apology, cuts off in heavy traffic, and generally ignores.

A common Chinese criticism of Westerners is that they don't go far enough out of their way for friends, yet they inexplicably treat strangers with extreme courtesy. The converse is true of the Western view of Chinese. Chinese tend to go all out for those within their own circles, sometimes putting themselves at great inconvenience or even in ethically questionable circumstances to do a favor for them. But Chinese treat strangers almost as if they did not exist. There is a callousness about their view of those outside the circle and precious little sense of civic responsibility toward them.

For example, if a person slips in a public place in the West, or has an accident on the street, most commonly some stranger or other will stop to help the person out. This is not universally true, of course, but helping others in distress is a trait with which we Westerners like to credit ourselves. Chinese, by contrast, routinely decline to get involved in such situations. Where there is no formal obligation to help out, the best tack is just to keep moving and not get involved—and most do.

I once witnessed a terrible traffic accident outside of Beijing in which a truck that was clearly out of control grazed against our car before it passed us and turned over quite violently just ahead of us on the road. A passenger in our car jumped out immediately—not to see if the truck driver was alive, but rather to determine the extent of the damage done to our car. When I approached the dazed truck driver, who it turned out was not seriously injured, I was told to stay away from him because he was probably drunk.

For another example, consider the Chinese attitude toward charity. There is no strong tradition of philanthropy in China, and where it is to be seen at all it is usually the province of the very rich. Beggars on the streets of Beijing and Shanghai know better than to waste too much time going after recalcitrant local citizens. They may beg from other Chinese, but they prefer to spend most of their energies on foreigners. This is not merely because they believe foreigners have a lot of money, but also because they have learned that there is a greater chance of playing on their sympathies.

A normally good-natured Chinese friend of mine narrowed his eyes sharply when I asked him if he would consider giving alms to a clearly needy handicapped person we saw on the street in Beijing. His reaction was fast and furious: It was not his responsibility to help this man, but rather that of the Civil Affairs Bureau. He was undaunted by the fact that China has almost no welfare system to speak of. I know this man to be the sort of person who would give the shirt off his back to help a friend. But as far as this manifestly poverty-stricken stranger in the street was concerned, the milk of his human kindness was in short supply, indeed.

A corollary to this principle is a tendency on the part of the Chinese not to show a great deal of respect for public property. Money is spent, by and large, on improving one's own living space and one's own property, but not on maintaining the common hallways in one's building, still less the street outside. Apartment dwellers in China may live in lovely flats, but the stairwells and hallways most often resemble those of a New York tenement—dark, dirty, and generally not maintained. In Taiwan, you can tell when there has been a day off by the amount of litter strewn in the public parks. The near total lack of civic responsibility, to my mind, is explainable by the circle theory, because appropriate civic behavior requires a respect for others outside of the circle—something that is rare indeed in China.

Dr. Arthur H. Smith saw this trend equally clearly in the imperial China of 1894. "Not only do the Chinese feel no interest in that which belongs to the 'public,'" he wrote in *Chinese Characteristics*, "but all such property, if unprotected and available, is a mark for theft. Paving-stones are carried off for private use, and square rods of the brick facing to city walls gradually disappear. . . . It is a common observation among the Chinese that . . . there is no one so imposed upon and cheated as the Emperor," he added. In 1998, the victim might be the communist government and the currency Beijing manhole covers, but the phenomenon is certainly no less true.

A further distinction between Western and Chinese points of view on relationships can be seen in attitudes toward the family. In the West, family relationships tend to rise and fall for emotional reasons. If Westerners provide for family members, it is usually more out of love than out of obligation, especially when the relationship is a more distant one. Chinese are motivated by emotions, too, but obligations tend to come first, and it is often more a function of form than content. It is not unthinkable or even uncommon for a Chinese couple to leave a child with grandparents to raise for many years if the business world requires them to live outside of China, for example. Couples will even separate and live in different cities; as long as the family is technically intact, the negative emotional effects of the separation can be managed.

Class Distinctions

There has never been anything particularly egalitarian about Chinese society—even under orthodox communism—and one's place in the hierarchy directly influences how one treats others and expects to be treated oneself. The sage Confucius, as noted in the previous chapter, detailed several principles of behavior that characterize civilized people. But people tend to be judged less by their depth of understanding or commitment to these principles than by how well their observable behavior reflects the principles. The importance of "keeping to the program" was underscored by the sage when he wrote, in the *Analects*, "Without an acquaintance with the rules of propriety, it is impossible for the character to be established." That is, manners make the man.

For example, it matters relatively little to a Chinese whether someone likes or dislikes an aged relative. What is important is how well Auntie is actually treated by her family. If she is alone or infirm, has she been invited to live with younger relatives who can care for her? Does she want for money? Do people visit her from time to time? Do they bring food or cash? A person's level of filial piety is assessed according to just such kinds of overt behavior. As noted above, it's form over content. One's private feelings hardly enter the picture at all; it all boils down to how thoroughly one honors one's obligations.

It is a system in which the rich and powerful are seen to be deserving of an extra measure of deference, which often expresses itself in fairly obsequious terms—particularly flattery, the doing of favors and the giving of gifts.

Socialism and its obsession with class struggle notwithstanding, class structure actually survived the Chinese revolution pretty much intact, even though there were clearly some changes in the lineup, with those who had been on top in the old society not necessarily faring well in the new China. Respect and deference that had been due to court officials and landlords before the revolution attached itself pretty naturally to the new communist overlords, who after all held the power and controlled the property in the new society. Party bureaucrats, for their part, lost little time in commandeering for themselves the trappings of power—better-quality apartments, chauffeur-driven limousines, and the rest. And this fact was not lost on the masses. Many people quickly recognized the new social order and lost little time in becoming appropriately obsequious.

Foreigners, who do not fit into the Chinese social system, tend for the most part to be accorded fairly high status by Chinese people, perhaps as a reflection of their standing as guests in China, or even more likely because they are generally perceived as well-to-do. As individuals of high status, they merit respectful treatment, which many accept as their due when they are in China, where normal treatment can often be unpleasant and uncomfortable. This tends to be most true of Caucasian foreigners and those who come from developed countries, however, as some Chinese view third-world foreigners as inferior.

Some foreigners adapt well to this sort of favorable treatment based on perceived class; others, particularly Americans, sometimes find it an affront to their egalitarian sensibilities. Refusing special treatment generally doesn't work very well, however, and foreigners who try to ignore class distinctions often find it frustrating. For example, the business executive who tries to befriend his driver or his maid may simply wind up making both of them uncomfortable. The driver doesn't necessarily desire a greater degree of equality with the boss, and may be far more relaxed when the foreign boss sits in the backseat of the car where he or she belongs than when the boss moves up to the front.

Nonverbal Communication

After dealing with the Chinese for any length of time, you will probably find that they have some habits that may offend or puzzle you.

First of all, due perhaps to the density of China's population, the Chinese conception of the proper social distance between people in a room, or in an elevator, is somewhat closer than that common to many Western cultures, especially America. Don't be surprised if you find a Chinese friend standing a bit too close to you for comfort, touching you, or breathing directly into your face when talking with you. You may even notice that as you step backward to adjust the distance to what you believe is a more suitable level, your Chinese counterpart may advance accordingly. I haven't ever found an effective way to extricate myself from this pas de deux; during conversations with certain Chinese friends I occasionally find myself in more or less constant backward motion.

Traditionally, Chinese were seldom demonstrative with members of the opposite sex in public; even husband and wife seldom touched when walking together on the street, or elsewhere in the public eye. This has changed on both sides of the Taiwan Strait. While older, more conservative people may still share this prejudice, younger Chinese can now frequently be seen holding hands and even embracing in public places. Foreigners should keep in mind the traditional viewpoint when traveling in mainland China or Taiwan; you may hold hands with a companion, but are well advised to avoid more passionate forms of contact. And when dealing with the Chinese, you should not touch a member of the opposite sex you do not know extremely well, except for a handshake. Other types of physical contact can be misinterpreted.

You may find it surprising that it is perfectly acceptable among the Chinese to be physical with members of the same sex. It is common for someone to be seen touching or leaning on a friend of the same sex, or even holding hands walking down the street, though generally nothing much more intimate than this. You may often feel yourself nudged through a door or tugged down a street by a Chinese friend. Among the Chinese on the mainland and elsewhere in Asia there is no taboo against this type of contact among people of the same sex; only somewhat Westernized Chinese may feel a bit self-conscious in such situations. And you should also be aware that there are no sexual overtones to this type of physical contact among the Chinese.

Some Chinese habits may be offensive to foreigners. Belching and spitting on the street, for example, are seen in China as natural if somewhat inelegant functions; they are not viewed as disgusting, especially by less educated Chinese. Though the government is trying to discourage such habits as spitting and littering by fining violators, they remain quite common, especially outside large cities. Passing gas is considered improper in polite company in China, and urban Chinese mothers will shame their children for doing it. But among less educated or less sophisticated Chinese it can occur unabashedly in public.

Many Chinese smoke cigarettes, and there is relatively low awareness that smoking in certain places may be offensive to nonsmokers, though this is growing, as many Chinese cities have prohibited smoking in public places. The regulation is generally honored in the breach, however. It remains unusual for someone to ask a Chinese not to smoke during a meeting or banquet or in a public place. If you need to do this, it's a good idea to couch it in terms of an allergy; this makes it easier to understand.

Non-Asian visitors to China, especially to the more remote areas, should also expect to be stared at occasionally. Gaping at someone is not viewed by the Chinese as an aggressive action, or even a particularly objectionable practice. If you are unusual in any way—because you are blond, or tall, or wearing odd-looking clothing, or obviously handicapped in some way—Chinese are very likely to gawk. They may even point you out to their children or friends. Being stared at as you stand in a department store trying on a piece of clothing can leave you feeling more like an animal in a zoo than an honored visitor, but you should keep in mind that the Chinese mean no harm by this. It's simply a cultural difference.

Conversely, sometimes in private situations Chinese will avoid meeting your eyes, even during conversation. This is usually a sign of shyness or embarrassment, and should not be confused with insincerity. In addition, Chinese often do not smile when they are introduced to strangers. This should not be taken for dissatisfaction, anger, or unfriendliness; it has far more to do with being socialized to keep feelings in rather than express them.

Another puzzling and often misinterpreted piece of public behavior is the Chinese propensity to laugh at a mishap. Many foreign visitors to China who have happened to trip on a curb or lose their footing on a slick floor have been infuriated to find themselves sitting on the ground, surrounded by giggling Chinese bystanders who make no effort to help them up. What you need to understand is that you are not really the butt of a joke; laughter, in addition to being a response to a humorous situation, is also one way the Chinese have of dealing with uncomfortable situations in which they are uncertain how to respond. And if no one steps forward to help it is probably only because of hesitancy to approach a foreigner, or fear of taking responsibility in what could prove to be a dicey situation.

Finally, you should know how to interpret a very typical

Chinese behavior that is also shared by the Japanese—the sucking in of air between clenched teeth. It generally follows a request that a Chinese finds difficult to satisfy. It is used to buy a little time while reflecting, but if you hear it, it's a good idea to jump in and modify or even retract the plea. Not to do so would likely place your Chinese host in the difficult position of having to say no to you.

The knife cuts both ways. Some of the things you may do quite naturally can drive the Chinese up a wall. Many an American businessman has mortified a Chinese acquaintance after a long separation with a bear-hug greeting at their reunion. The slap on the back, the mock punch, and other types of rough handling common among American men in particular are simply not done in China, especially among relative strangers, and the Chinese don't know how to react to them. Some Chinese, particularly older ones, can also be strongly offended when guests touch members of the opposite sex in ways that to them seem suggestive. You must also not be physically demonstrative with those who are much older or who rank much higher than yourself.

Bear in mind also that postures can be important. Don't slink down in your chair or put your feet up on the table when you are meeting with a Chinese, lest he or she feel you are not being properly respectful. And never, never point to something with your head or your foot, still less use your foot to manipulate something; using a body part other than your hands to make such a gesture is considered uncouth. When handing an object—like a teacup, or a business card—to someone else, especially someone of higher rank, use both hands, not just one. This is a sign of respect.

Then there is a whole set of gestures that simply are misinterpreted because they are different. "Come here," signaled in the West by curling your index finger upward toward yourself, is not understood by the Chinese; they communicate the same concept by extending an outstretched hand facedown and waving it up and down. To Westerners that gesture looks like a good-bye wave. A shrug of the shoulders doesn't necessarily communicate "I don't know" to a Chinese; to many it just looks like bad posture. Don't try to give the "okay" sign with your thumb and forefinger forming a circle; you may well just get a blank stare (though paradoxically, a lot of Chinese understand what the English word "okay" means). And few of your Western-style obscene gestures will be understood per se, though the anger that engenders them will probably still be communicated.

There are, however, some universals. Nodding your head for agreement and shaking it for disagreement, for example, are completely understood by the Chinese, though "no" is also often expressed with a vigorous waving motion of the hand from side to side in front of the face. Pointing to your chest to signify yourself is also comprehended, though you may also occasionally see a Chinese pointing to his or her nose instead. Thumbs-up communicates approval in both cultures. And clapping your hands is a universal way of applauding; the only twist in mainland China is that the objects of applause always clap back at the audience as a reciprocal expression of appreciation. You won't usually see this in Hong Kong, Taiwan, or Singapore.

It is fair to say that Chinese are far more comfortable with silence than are Westerners. Many business executives who visit China find themselves talking too much during meetings, simply because they are uncomfortable with even a pregnant pause. Silence can be a virtue among Chinese, for it often signifies reflection and assessment of a situation. In fact, some Chinese accuse Westerners of being far more apt than they themselves to say things spontaneously that turn out to be ill advised or incorrect.

Silence can also be a sign of politeness, a signal that you have the complete attention of your Chinese listener, who is waiting for you to continue. But it can also be a ploy, used by Chinese negotiators to buy time and, in so doing, to ferret out the position of their counterparts.

Communication among Chinese is often far more subtle than it is among foreigners. What is left unsaid is easily as important as what is expressed directly, and silence at a well-chosen moment can speak volumes. This is not to say that lengthy periods of no conversation are desirable or even common. To the extent that they signify that two people are uncomfortable with one another or can't think of things to talk about, they are of course quite awkward. The natural tendency is to try to make conversation, and the Chinese will do so, too. Just don't confuse such a situation with one in which someone is pausing to mull over a point, waiting for someone else to respond to a question, or deliberately *not* agreeing with a statement that has been made. Learn also to judge whose silence it really is. If your counterpart holds the floor, it is his or her silence, and you need not concern yourself with trying to break it.

Saying No

Refusing a request made by a guest is considered an unacceptable form of behavior among Chinese everywhere. Being turned down to your face causes *you* to lose face, and no good Chinese host ever wants to put his guests in such a position. This is why you should never press a point with your host that is likely to force him or her to say no. If cornered, Chinese people will eventually tell you that no is no; they will wonder all the time why you insisted on pressing the point, however, since the face that is lost in the process is your own.

To save everyone's face, the Chinese have devised a number of methods of refusing without actually saying no. The most common is to say that to grant the wish would be "inconvenient." Unless you are dealing with a very close friend, don't take this at face value. But neither should you take it as a signal to try to convince the host that the obstacles can be surmounted and it isn't really as inconvenient as it may seem. "Inconvenient" may mean that there are political problems associated with fulfilling a request that a Chinese would rather not have to explain fully. Ultimately, in response to a request or a negotiated demand, "inconvenient" means no, and if you're smart you won't press the point.

Another common tack is to say that a request is "under consideration" or "being discussed." This response can occasionally be taken at face value, but it generally means that something is unlikely to happen, or at very least that there is no way a "yes" response can be given at the current time. Saying that something is being considered puts the whole problem off; it gets the host out of a tight situation in the current meeting by excluding the topic from further discussion. Still another way of handling an ungrantable request is not to deal with it at all. In both cases the hope is that you will read the handwriting on the wall and back away quietly, never raising the point again.

Another favorite way out is to blame someone else for the roadblock. Accomplishing anything in the PRC generally takes cooperation among different government units; if you don't want to grant a request, it's always pretty easy to find a scapegoat somewhere else in the vast bureaucracy.

Finally, a Chinese may even tell a lie to avoid saying no or some other breach of surface harmony, inventing a story that has absolutely no truth to it just to get out of the uncomfortable position in which he or she feels placed. A colleague of mine once requested and received permission to visit a Chinese arms factory, but as the day of the visit approached the host organization had second thoughts about the propriety of allowing a Westerner in to view such a sensitive installation. Rather than own up to the truth, the Chinese escort officer simply told the foreign guest that the factory was closed on the appointed day. Although this was a case of a Chinese lying to cover up his unit's own mistake, lying sometimes isn't as dishonorable as it may seem on the surface. Equally often the reason for all the machinations is in fact the wish to spare a guest a loss of face.

Recap: A Dozen Points on Etiquette

1. Manners for the Chinese are more a matter of form than substance. They have as much to do with fulfilling obligations and avoiding criticism as they do kindness and solicitousness per se.
2. Maintaining surface harmony at all times is of paramount importance to Chinese people. Regardless of one's true feelings, one should never do anything to

cause a moment of public unpleasantness or embarrassment.

3. The need to preserve surface harmony and face often causes the Chinese to use intermediaries to carry unpleasant news. There is no premium on confrontation. Intermediaries play an important role in business, where they are used to float trial balloons and communicate bad news, and serve as back channels for information.
4. Relatives, friends, neighbors, classmates, and co-workers are all people to whom one bears some form of obligation. No obligation is felt to others outside of one's circle, which explains the paucity of philanthropy in China and the tendency on the part of the Chinese to show little respect for public property or commonly held property.
5. Chinese society—communist and otherwise—has always had its class distinctions. Respect and deference are due to those in superior positions. Foreigners, whether they seek it or not, tend to be accorded fairly high status.
6. The Chinese conception of the proper social distance between people is different from the Western conception; Chinese people often stand too close for Western tastes.
7. Traditional Chinese are never demonstrative in public, though today's younger generation often violates this taboo. Chinese are more prone to touching among members of the same sex, which has no particular sexual connotations.
8. Chinese habits some Westerners experience as offensive include belching and expectorating on the street, smoking cigarettes indiscriminately, and staring at foreigners. Chinese laughter at mishaps is a commonly misunder-

stood behavior. It signals not humor but rather discomfort and hesitancy.

9. Foreigners can offend Chinese counterparts with physically demonstrative behavior, including touching Chinese of the opposite sex or of advanced age or high rank. Slinking in one's chair and pointing to objects with a body part other than one's hands are considered uncouth. Gestures not commonly understood by Chinese include curling the index finger to signify "Come here," shrugging the shoulders to signify "I don't know," and using several obscene gestures easily understood in the West.
10. Chinese are far more comfortable with silence than Westerners. It can be a sign of politeness, signifying that one is paying attention, but it can also be a ploy to buy time or draw the other party's position out in a negotiation.
11. The Chinese have devised a number of methods of refusing something without exactly saying no. These include saying something is "inconvenient," "under consideration," or "being discussed." Still another way of handling an ungrantable request is not to deal with it at all.
12. A Chinese may tell a lie to avoid a breach of social harmony. Lying sometimes isn't as dishonorable as it may seem on the surface. It can be used simply to spare a guest a loss of face.

Chapter VI

The Business Meeting

WHETHER YOU ARE RECEIVED BY A VICE PREMIER OR A prison warden, or whether you visit a factory, a kindergarten, a commune, or the Great Hall of the People, you should not be surprised to find striking similarity in the way the meetings are conducted. Chinese meetings follow a protocol all their own no matter what the setting, and understanding their rhythm can help you to read signals more clearly.

ARRANGING THE MEETING

First of all, setting up a meeting in the PRC often takes more than a simple phone call or fax, and can in fact be quite an involved process, especially if a government organization is involved. If it is the Western party who requests the meeting, and if that party is not well known to the Chinese organization with whom the conference is being sought, the Chinese may be loath to agree to a face-to-face parley without further information. Just as Chinese individuals prefer to be formally introduced to new people, Chinese organizations want some background information about their counterparts before they agree to formal discussions.

The first order of business is thus to establish your credentials. This may be accomplished through an introduction by a third party known to both parties—either an individual or an organization—or you can act for yourself. It's best to provide as much background information as possible in the initial overture—preferably in written form. Also provide information about the topic you wish to discuss, and give the Chinese side some time to study the request. This is especially necessary if a high-level meeting is being sought.

If it is the Chinese side that requested the meeting in the first place, there will be less trouble all around, for the homework will have already been done. It is perfectly acceptable in this case to ask your Chinese counterparts for as much advance information as possible prior to the meeting, so you can learn more about what it is they hope to accomplish and prepare your own positions.

There are two good reasons that the Chinese prefer—and often insist on—advance information. First of all, they dislike surprises. Knowing up front what the other party wishes to discuss enables them to hammer out their own positions, and to approach the meeting with the confidence that they have the benefit of the collective wisdom of the "departments concerned," as they like to put it.

This approach goes against the Western grain to a certain extent. Westerners often prefer to be present when an idea is first introduced in order to make the best case for it and to gauge the reaction of their counterparts firsthand. But the

Chinese don't work that way; if ambushed they will simply listen and defer the matter for later consideration. You'll seldom see a Chinese leader make an off-the-cuff decision during a meeting with a foreigner unless it is on a matter of relatively little importance.

The second reason that it is helpful to tip your hand in advance of a meeting is that this maximizes the chance of the Chinese side lining up the correct attendees. If a Chinese ministry or corporation is asked to meet with a foreign executive and the topic is not spelled out clearly in advance, chances are good that responsibility for attending the meeting and reporting back will devolve on the "external affairs section" of the Chinese organization.

This department, staffed by what one wag has referred to as "barbarian handlers," makes no major decisions of its own, performing instead a basic liaison function. While the external affairs section can serve as a useful means of identifying the proper decision-maker within the organization, going this route can also waste valuable time. A little advance information can short-circuit the process and result in accomplishing the same thing in less time.

A Chinese organization will sometimes agree in principle to a meeting but will resist setting a time for it, or specifying exactly who will attend. This is especially true if the request comes well in advance of the desired meeting date, or if the meeting is being sought on behalf of individuals who have not yet arrived in China. The PRC is a place where final arrangements are frequently made at the last minute. A Chinese leader who commits to a specific time weeks in advance of a meeting loses the flexibility to engage in other, possibly more important, activities that may present themselves in the intervening period. Then, too, the Chinese feel that until someone actually arrives in town there is no hurry to set up a meeting time; any of a million things could happen to delay or cancel the trip.

This is why it is often the case that you can arrive in China to find that none of the half dozen meetings you requested months in advance has in fact yet been set up. The Chinese penchant for last-minute arrangements can be maddening in its uncertainty. The good news is that these things have a way of working themselves out, and most of the meetings generally wind up getting on the agenda somehow. The bad news is that the route to getting the meeting pinned down may involve an ulcer or two on your part.

This is also why meetings with extremely high-ranking officials in China—minister level and above—are almost never pinned down until the day before, or even the day of the event. Such meetings also have a way of occurring on the very last day of a foreign delegation's visit to Beijing. I've often suspected that keeping these audiences indefinite until the last moment serves a number of purposes: It creates suspense and a feeling of gratitude toward the host organization on the part of foreign guests, who perceive the hosts as coming through at the last minute for them. It's also a form of manipulation; a way of rewarding foreigners for doing something the Chinese desire them to do. And they aren't above doing this to extremely high-ranking guests, including foreign ministers and corporate CEOs.

The good news is that while meetings with government officials may be stage-managed in these ways, meetings with Chinese corporate officials are getting more and more informal. The new breed of confident, experienced Chinese corporate executives is increasingly dispensing with some of the more formal aspects of the protocol and simply getting down to business.

THE SETUP

It's unlikely you will attend a meeting in the office of a Chinese official, though this does happen from time to time. Offices tend to be crowded and rather dreary places in China, at least in government buildings, and a small room with several desks, uncomfortable chairs, and one or two ringing telephones is not considered a fitting place to receive guests. The fact that stray papers bearing purported state secrets may be lying around is the ostensible reason many Chinese government organizations actually prohibit foreigners from entering working offices.

Most often, meetings are held in rooms furnished solely for this purpose. They may be located down the hall from the office or in a contiguous building. In government buildings these rooms are usually fitted out with the ubiquitous overstuffed chairs and sofas you see throughout China—the same type of furniture visible in the photos of Richard Nixon's reception in Chairman Mao's study in 1972. The chairs, which line the perimeter of the room, are generally draped with drab seat covers and antimacassars, and are interspersed with coffee tables and end tables. Alternatively, there may be an oblong table in the center of the room with straight chairs arranged all around it, rather like a spartan conference room. In Chinese business establishments, you will probably still be ushered into a meeting room, but it is more likely to be a comfortable, Western-style setup.

It is very important to arrive at a meeting on time in the PRC. Punctuality is considered a virtue on the mainland as well as in Taiwan, and keeping others waiting is seen as impolite. If you happen to arrive late to a meeting, be sure to apologize; this is a signal that you intended no slight by your tardiness. Nor is it appropriate to arrive too early for a meeting. A Chinese delegation I escorted around the United States once arrived fifteen minutes early at the headquarters of a company with which they had scheduled a meeting. Rather than go in and embarrass their unprepared hosts, they insisted that the driver cruise around the block until the appointed hour.

Meeting formalities begin with the arrival of the guests at the site. It is considered important that guests be greeted upon their arrival and escorted to the meeting room. The principal host need not go down to the street to meet the cars, but he or she should send a representative to do this. It is considered good form for the host to be in the meeting room waiting when the guests arrive. The highest-ranking guest should ideally enter the room first; if he or she does not, there is a risk that the Chinese host will mistake whoever *does* enter first—whether a secretary or a low-level functionary—for the head person. Chinese delegations tend to enter rooms in something approaching protocol order, with the first- and second-ranking delegates leading the way. Only interpreters typically break rank, since they are necessary to help the leaders communicate. So, extrapolating from their own procedures, Chinese will expect the leader to come in first. But again, in business meetings rather than government meetings, people are less and less likely to stand on this much ceremony.

After hands are shaken all around, guests are escorted to seats. Only in very formal meetings is the seating rigid; guests are seated in descending order of rank and interpreters are placed behind the principal speakers. Most meetings are more informal, however, even though there is always a certain protocol that governs where the most important people are placed.

The principal guest and other VIP guests are generally escorted by the principal host to seats of honor. In rooms in which chairs are arranged along the perimeter, the place of honor is the seat to the host's immediate right on a sofa or in chairs at the end of the room opposite the door. Other high-ranking guests are shown to seats in the same general area of the room, and the interpreter is seated strategically near the host and the principal guest. Other guests are left to their own devices to seat themselves, though if you hesitate you may be directed to a seat by a solicitous Chinese. Only after the guests have selected seats will the balance of the Chinese participants seat themselves (see Figure 2).

If the meeting room has a large central table, the principal guest may be seated directly opposite the main host rather than to his or her right. Other members of the delegations fill in the other seats. Only in formal meetings and negotiations do all members of the Chinese delegation sit on one side of the table and foreigners line the other. In this situation, the lowest-ranking delegation members are seated at the ends of the table, farthest from the principals. In less formal situations, the sides need not be so assiduously segregated, but it is still the case that principals sit at the center (see Figure 3).

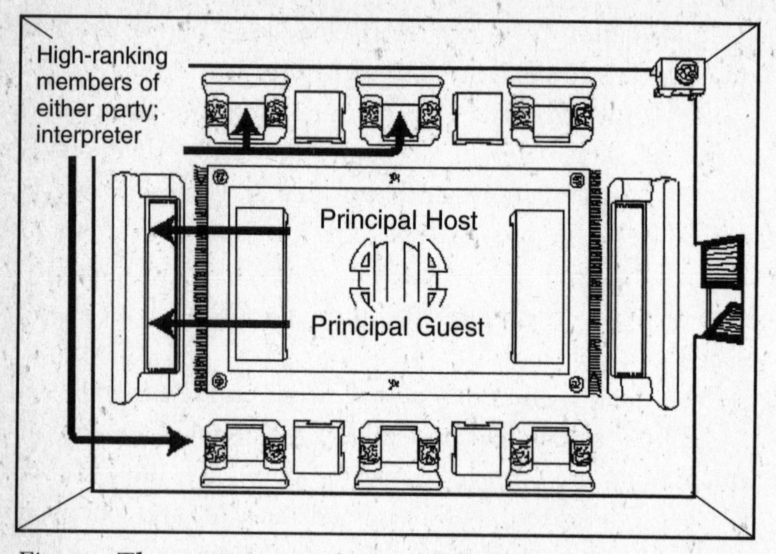

Figure 2. ***The arrangement of a typical Chinese meeting room.*** *The principal guest is seated at the principal host's right on a sofa or in chairs opposite the door. Other high-ranking guests are seated in the immediate vicinity, as are interpreters.*

The Course of the Meeting

Most Chinese gatherings begin with small talk, especially when the host and guests do not know one another well. The purpose is to get acquainted and make preliminary assessments of each other before any business is discussed. The Chinese are, in general, more patient in business dealings than their Western counterparts, and they tend to recoil from the Western "Lay-all-your-cards-on-the-table" approach when they do not know people well. Important business dealings are to be undertaken only with those one trusts, and trust is not something that can be established in too short a period of time.

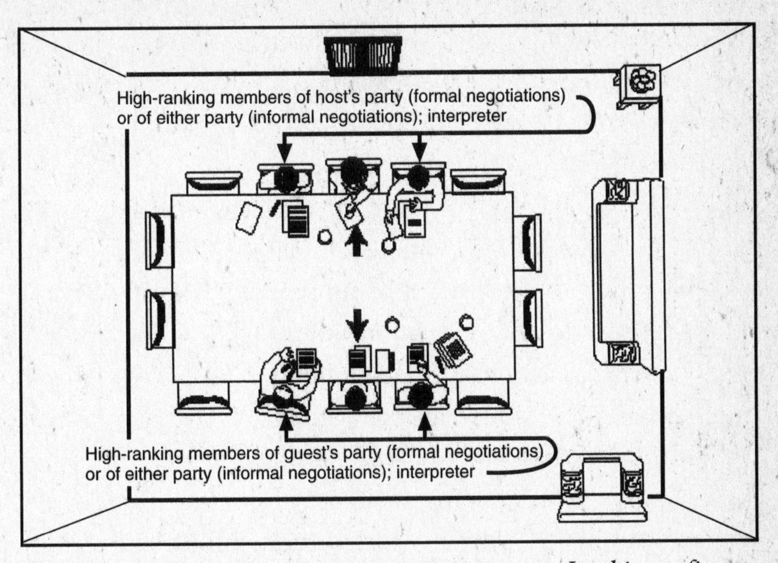

Figure 3. ***A variant meeting room arrangement****. In this configuration, individuals are seated around a large conference table. The principal guest is seated opposite the principal host. High-ranking guests and interpreters are seated in the immediate vicinity.*

It's important, then, not to come in swinging, but to establish the foundation of a relationship and build slowly. There is no need to rush into a discussion of business; the topic will come up naturally in time. Start out with icebreakers like general observations or questions. The Chinese are apt to bring up the weather ("You have brought good weather with you, Mr. Smith") or the minutiae of your trip to China (for example, whether your plane arrived on time, what sights of interest you have already seen in the city, whether you have eaten a particular local delicacy) before any issue of substance is broached. For your part, feel free to ask if the host has ever visited your country, how long he or she has been with the organization or held the present position, and so on. From there you can move on to more substantive, but still safe, territory, such as what the host's area of responsibility is within his ministry, organization, or corporation. Usually the matter at hand will find its way into the conversation this way.

Chinese officials seldom attend meetings with foreigners alone; as a matter of policy there is usually a retinue of lesser-ranking functionaries and staff members on hand as well. Even in very small-scale meetings there is invariably at least one other person present. Occasionally the Chinese do not even bother to introduce all the participants at the start of a meeting. It is usually quite clear why certain individuals are invited; they may have some say in the business at hand, be responsible for liaison with the foreign guest, or be charged with essential tasks such as translating or note-taking.

But equally often there are others present who have no apparent reason for being there. It was once thought that sometimes true decision-makers went deliberately unidentified, eager to make a firsthand assessment of the foreign guest but happy to leave the task of running the meeting and formally receiving the guests to someone of lower rank, but this in fact is seldom if ever true. If there are unnamed participants, it is far more likely that they are there as observers or apprentices, and so the Chinese leader does not think it is important to introduce them.

Discussions with Chinese officials are not free-for-all exchanges; they are structured dialogues between principals on both sides that are witnessed by an assemblage of others. Participants other than the principal host and guest—and perhaps one or two other very high-ranking members of the group—are present for the entire meeting, but they seldom participate in the conversation, and then only upon explicit invitation. Most do not participate at all.

The principal host will probably begin with a short welcoming speech after the initial formalities are over. If the Chinese have asked for the meeting, the host will probably state the business at hand as part of his or her opening remarks. If the meeting is being held at the behest of the guest, then after the welcome the host will turn the floor over to the principal guest to begin the substantive discussion.

In general, the Chinese prefer to be in the position of reacting to others' ideas rather than bearing the onus of setting the scope of the discussion themselves. On one level this can be seen as a courtesy—letting the guest speak first is basic good manners. But sometimes more is at work here than just regard for etiquette. In matters relating to international business, and especially aspects of it that may be new to China, even Chinese leaders may feel a certain amount of insecurity. This is due, no doubt, to the fact that the PRC was cut off from the rest of the world during a vitally important period in the development and maturation of international commerce.

Some Chinese, particularly those from the hinterlands, do not fully understand all of the intricacies of foreign trade, and they are smart enough to know it. So allowing the guest to frame the conversation and put forth proposals permits them to avert the possibility of saying something foolish or naïve. It also has the added benefits of getting the foreign guests to tip their hands first, and of providing a bit of time to consider what they have to say and to react to it.

Chinese listeners will often punctuate the remarks of other speakers with nods or affirmative grunts. These may come as often as every sentence or two. What they mean is, "I have heard you," or "I have understood what you are saying." These ejaculations do *not* mean "I agree with you" or "I give my assent," and should never be taken as such. Many serious misunderstandings have resulted from foreigners' mistaking this sort of signal for accord or permission.

During a meeting, it is always important to keep in mind who holds the floor at any given time. Remember that these meetings are not free exchanges but rather structured conversations; there is a rhythm at work. Typically, if you are the person who states the business, you have two alternatives: You may put the entire question on the table in all of its complexity, or you can break the subject down into parts.

In the first instance, you may begin by speaking for a full five or ten minutes without interruption as you lay out the intricacies of the issue at hand, and catalog your organization's positions on all of the components that need to be discussed. In the context of a discussion of the impediments to a joint venture, for example, you might bring up financing requirements and quality control as the major areas of concern. Once you have finished this, it is your counterpart's turn to speak to all of these issues. The Chinese are diligent about following the flow of such expositions, and in their responses will generally touch meticulously on all of the points raised.

Alternatively, you may define the issue and then raise the component points individually. You may actually enumerate the points to be discussed, saying at the outset, for example, that you intend to cover six important considerations. In this case your counterpart is free to speak to each point as it is brought up, with you reclaiming the floor each time a point has been fully discussed to raise the next one. There need be no mystery about which approach a speaker chooses to take; it is good form, in fact, to make clear up front whether you intend to talk about the whole subject or deal with it piecemeal. Flagging it in this way helps everyone to know whose turn it is to speak at any given time.

Regardless of how you choose to structure your remarks, remember to keep them brief and to the point. Preparing them in advance is a wise move. It's best to say what you have come to say and then to stop talking, giving up the floor to your counterpart.

It is important to know who holds the floor because it is considered rude to interrupt a speaker while he or she is talking. An occasional short intervention is acceptable—it is fine, for example, to fill in a relevant piece of information that may not be known to the speaker. But you must not break in and speak so long that you effectively reclaim the floor. Since "ownership" of the floor is not typically a major concern in Western-style meetings, it is important that you monitor your own behavior in this regard when dealing with the Chinese.

Another cardinal rule of conduct during meetings is never to put anyone on the spot, at least not in person. This means, for example, never placing someone in the position of having to divulge information he or she seems unwilling to discuss, or to challenge someone on a particular point. You should always offer a way out so that your counterpart can preserve face. On the other hand, you can often be more frank in written form. Sometimes a well-crafted follow-up letter can make important points that would have been awkward to make in a face-to-face discussion.

Count on the Chinese to take detailed notes of proceedings and to circulate them to all interested parties; don't be surprised if someone not at the initial meeting appears fully informed about the proceedings at some later time. You can also count on the Chinese side to retrieve these notes and quote them back to you chapter and verse if subsequent events cast any doubt on what was said—provided that consulting the record advances the Chinese position in the matter at hand. Foreign companies with short institutional memories, due either to frequent changes in personnel or simply to bad record-keeping, are thus at a disadvantage in China—a point worth considering when you are structuring negotiating teams and establishing negotiating procedures.

Using Interpreters

While these days it is more common than ever before to run into Chinese managers and high-level bureaucrats who speak foreign languages fluently enough to conduct business, in the vast majority of cases international business is still transacted through interpreters. Even managers who speak foreign languages frequently prefer to use interpreters anyway, in order to save face, buy time, or simply speak more fluently. Chinese organizations with dealings abroad can be relied on to have access to interpreters who speak English, Japanese, Russian, and even German and French.

It often makes sense to bring your own interpreter to China, but it is not essential to do so for protocol purposes. For complicated negotiations your own interpreter can be worth his or her weight in gold in communicating sophisticated legal and technical concepts in intricate detail, as well as in reporting back on discussions that take place in Chinese among the negotiators themselves. Some business representatives favor bringing along their own translators to ensure that they are not hoodwinked by one who is partial to the Chinese position. In fact, while clarity is a sound reason to hire your own interpreter, self-defense is probably not. It is the job of any translator to communicate clearly in both languages, and you are far more likely to bump into an incompetent interpreter in China than to meet one who is actively trying to deceive you.

Sometimes a good interpreter can even save you from yourself. Foreigners sometimes say things thoughtlessly that would offend Chinese hosts if they were translated directly—such as calling the host by the wrong name or title or referring to China by an outdated name (see "Drinking and Toasting" in Chapter 8). In such situations, a crackerjack interpreter will correct the remark as it is translated, thus saving face for all concerned.

A friend of mine reports a situation in which an interpreter preserved the peace during a difficult negotiation by watering down some heated remarks by a Chinese party. The dispute centered over whether a Chinese enterprise that wanted to import some vehicles could lower the price by manufacturing one of the key component parts by itself. The foreign manufacturer wanted to discourage this, since it would not be economical to do so given the small number of units the Chinese enterprise wanted to purchase. The Chinese side, however, assumed that his reluctance bespoke an unjustified lack of confidence in China's manufacturing ability.

"We know how to manufacture nuclear weapons, so don't you think we can manage to put together your crappy little articulation joint?" sneered an irate engineer on the Chinese side. The entire Chinese side sat frozen, waiting to see how the interpreter was going to translate *that.* But she didn't miss a beat. "I think Engineer Wang feels the part is well within the scope of what they can handle," she announced, thus averting an otherwise assured impasse in the negotiations.

Don't expect a member of your team to do double duty as a substantive contributor to the discussion *and* an interpreter. To use someone as a translator is for all practical purposes to lose that person's services as a negotiator, since interpreting is hard work and takes a good deal of quick thought and concentration. Be sensitive, too, to the fact that a team member who is of Chinese extraction or who speaks Chinese may not wish to be seen by the Chinese as an interpreter, especially if he or she is on the team because of a different area of expertise. The person's face may be at stake here.

When you bring your own interpreter, the custom is that he or she translates your remarks, and the one supplied by the Chinese side translates the remarks of your Chinese counterpart. When there is only one interpreter, obviously, the person serves as the voice of both principal host *and* principal guest.

There are ways of assessing how good a job the interpreter is doing even if you don't speak both languages. A sure sign of a pro is lack of hesitation on his or her part and obvious ease in expressing thoughts in both languages. A good interpreter will also occasionally query you if you use an expression he or she doesn't understand. This often happens when you use slang. On the other hand, if the questions or answers coming from the Chinese don't seem to track with your remarks, if the technical terms create delays and seem to pose insurmountable problems, or if other bilingual members of the Chinese group are constantly offering corrections or filling in blanks, chances are that the interpreter is in over his or her head.

Getting the Chinese to find a substitute for an inept interpreter is dicey business. You can't very well transmit this message through the interpreter in question; it must be done out of the person's hearing through some other liaison person. Since this is an assault on the interpreter's competence and hence his or her face, it is a serious matter. If a replacement is made, chances are good that the foreign delegation will never see the first interpreter again. On the other hand, doing this is preferable to conducting a series of inconclusive meetings characterized by miscommunication. By all means try to work with an interpreter who shows some competence and promise; but if the situation is beyond repair, don't hesitate to ask for a change. You don't really have a choice.

There is an art to talking through interpreters. The cardinal rule is to pause frequently, breaking your remarks up into bite-sized pieces. The longer you speak without stopping, the greater the likelihood something you say will be mistranslated, or not translated at all. One thought—one or two sentences—at a time is a good standard. This pace also allows you time between remarks to think through what you wish to say next.

Avoid slang and excessively colloquial expressions, which are often not understood at all. American English, for instance, boasts a number of expressive metaphors from the world of sports, but woe unto the English speaker who asks a Chinese for a "ballpark figure" or a "level playing field," or who expresses a fear of "striking out," not "getting to first base" or "being out in left field." It's a rare interpreter who has enough experience with the game of baseball to figure out such terms.

Many colloquialisms will simply be misunderstood, a worse fate than in the case of those that are not understood at all, since they stand an excellent chance of being translated literally. I remember, for example, one instance when a foreign businessman accused his Chinese partners of using a particular obstacle as a "red herring" for another problem. The translator's faithful and literal rendering of this remark succeeded only in bewildering the Chinese audience.

Another basic rule concerning the use of interpreters: Don't make the mistake of addressing your remarks directly to the translator. It's easy to fall into this trap, since speakers tend to be very aware of the fact that it is the interpreter and not their counterpart who is actually understanding what is being said in "real time." It is natural to study the face of the translator to be certain that he or she, at least, understands the nuances of your remarks. But you should fight the impulse. Focusing on the interpreter is impolite because it fails to accord proper respect to the Chinese host or guest.

Similarly, fight the all-too-common urge to deal with a situation in which you are not being understood by repeating your remarks at double volume. In 99 percent of the cases the problem is comprehension, not transmission. Don't shout; a far more effective solution is to come up with simpler words that convey the same idea. In fact, an effective tactic to use whenever you are not certain that your point got across is to say essentially the same thing using different words.

CONCLUDING A MEETING

Before a meeting is finished, it is an excellent idea to restate your understanding of exactly what was accomplished, or even to leave behind a set of minutes of the meeting that summarizes key points of agreement. This is an obvious but very worthwhile strategy for making sure that both sides agree on what happened and on what the next steps will be. If it is a first meeting, you can also ask the Chinese host—who, if he or she is a high-ranking official, will likely be difficult to reach in person in the future—to designate a contact person for future dealings. The Chinese are generally quite willing to do this, and it offers the practical advantage of continuity; you don't have to reinvent the wheel and bring a new contact person up to speed on the matter at hand each time you approach the Chinese organization about it.

It also serves an additional purpose. If a high-ranking cadre assigns to a staff member a responsibility such as future liaison with a foreign concern, it is a way of putting his or her imprimatur on the matters that have been discussed. It means that the relationship with you, or the issue under discussion, is a matter of personal concern, and it increases the likelihood that you will receive cooperation from the Chinese unit in the future.

It's usually fairly obvious when the business has been transacted and the meeting is over. As far as protocol is concerned, either side can end a meeting. The host may observe that the guests must be tired, or hungry, or must have important things to do with the rest of their day during their all-too-short visit to the city. Or the principal guest may point out that the group has already taken up a great deal of the host's time, and that they are grateful to him or her for spending the time with them. In either case, the host generally sends someone to escort the guests to their car; occasionally he or she will do the honors in person.

One final point: The Chinese are extremely punctual about eating times, and if a prelunch meeting is threatening to run long, don't be surprised if an adjournment is suggested by your counterpart. One Western observer therefore suggests that those few moments toward the end of a negotiation session before a meal are among the best times to press Chinese for concessions.

Recap: A Dozen Notes on Business Meetings

1. Chinese organizations typically request background information before they agree to formal discussions. Provide as much information as possible about the individuals who will be present, the organization you are representing, and the topic you wish to discuss, and give the Chinese side time to study the request.
2. The Chinese dislike surprises, preferring to hammer out their own positions in advance of a meeting. Knowing what will be discussed beforehand also permits them to select the proper participants for a meeting.
3. In China, meetings are generally held in conference rooms rather than offices. Chairs may line the perimeter of the room or may be arranged around an oblong table in the center. Seating is not rigid, but there typically are designated places for the principals.

4. Punctuality is considered a virtue, so it is important to arrive at a meeting on time—not late and not early. Guests are greeted upon arrival by a representative and escorted to the meeting room; hosts are expected to be in place before guests arrive.
5. Chinese generally expect foreign delegation leaders to enter a room first, and this prevents confusion. Important guests are escorted to seats, with the principal guest placed in a seat of honor. Others may sit where they like.
6. Chinese meetings begin with small talk. Avoid the temptation to lay your cards on the table at first; start out with icebreakers like general observations or questions.
7. Chinese officials seldom hold solo meetings with foreigners; as a matter of policy, staff members are invariably present. Not all participants are necessarily introduced; those who are not are usually observers or apprentices, however, not decision-makers or active participants.
8. Chinese meetings are structured dialogues between principals on both sides; others participate in the conversation only upon explicit invitation. The Chinese prefer to react to others' ideas, and not to bear the onus of setting the scope of the discussion themselves.
9. Chinese often signal the speaker with nods or interjections that they understand what he or she is saying. Such ejaculations do not necessarily signal agreement. Remember who holds the floor, and don't interrupt a speaker.
10. Never put anyone on the spot during a meeting. Always offer a way out so your counterpart can preserve face.

11. A good interpreter can help you immeasurably in China. When talking through an interpreter, pause frequently and avoid slang and colloquialisms. Always talk to the host, never directly to the translator.
12. Restate what was accomplished at the close of a meeting to guard against misunderstanding. Ask for a contact person for future dealings.

Chapter VII

Relationships with Foreigners

The Chinese View of Outsiders

DESPITE OUTBREAKS OF XENOPHOBIA THAT HAVE CHARACTERized various periods in Chinese history, the Chinese are an extremely hospitable people who frequently go far out of their way to make guests feel at home among them. While they may sometimes be rude and impolite to fellow countrymen they do not know, they are typically quite pleasant to Western visitors, who are obviously guests in their country. Don't be surprised if someone you hardly know—or even someone you meet on the street—offers you some tea, invites you out for a snack, or approaches you to practice a little English. This is the Confucian emphasis on hospitality at work.

There is nevertheless a certain schizophrenia involved in the Chinese view of Westerners, senses of inferiority and superiority that may curiously exist side by side. Lu Xun, a great twentieth-century Chinese writer, once quipped that through the ages the Chinese have either looked down on foreigners as brutes or up to them as saints, but have never actually been able to call them friends or speak of them as equals. On the one hand, the Chinese see Western society as highly advanced in many ways. They view its achievements in the development of science and technology, manufacturing, transportation, and agriculture, not to mention its significant economic accomplishments, as worthy of note, emulation, and even envy.

On the other hand, however, China has a proud, five-thousand-year history, and a civilization and culture the Chinese consider second to none. The Western world may well be more advanced materially, but many Chinese see it as clearly lacking in moral fiber—how else to explain the preponderance of drugs, illicit sex, and other degenerate conduct they read and hear about in the United States and elsewhere? By this reckoning, Westerners cannot possibly be the moral equals of Chinese. As far as many Chinese are concerned, when all is said and done, as far as their social customs are concerned, Westerners are ultimately not much better than barbarians. They don't understand the finer points of etiquette and can't necessarily be counted on to behave properly.

What this underscores is the propensity of the Chinese to judge Westerners and their behavior according to Chinese standards. For Chinese, there are relatively few choices as to what constitutes proper and improper behavior; they grow up imbued with very clear ideas of what is right and what is wrong. Lacking another set of standards, they can hardly be faulted for using this yardstick to judge others, even those not reared in their culture.

How much this tendency is actually expressed correlates

strongly with a Chinese person's station in life, and especially with level of education and geographical location. Rural Chinese, for example, who may lack sophistication and contact with the world outside of China, are more likely to view foreigners exclusively through Chinese lenses. Urbanized and educated Chinese, on the other hand, are far more apt to have experience with foreigners and thus to make allowances for cultural differences.

Excuses are frequently made for transgressions by foreign guests, known by the affectionate term *laowai* (old outsider), on the grounds that they don't know any better. There is a real double standard at work. It is the very fact that there are no expectations that foreigners will ever really measure up in the area of protocol and manners that is at issue here. It's precisely this condescending attitude that condemns Westerners to be termed little better than barbarians—the same classification used to describe the Mongolian hordes who pillaged northern China for many hundreds of years—especially when the Chinese are angry with them. On the other hand, the fact that expectations are so low also affords a significant opportunity for Westerners. If you display *some* knowledge of Chinese customs, however small, you can easily earn accolades and admiration.

Foreigners should approach China knowing that no matter how long they stay or how well they learn the language and the customs, they will always be considered different. There is basically no such thing as ever really blending in completely. While the Chinese generally respect an outsider who has a knowledge of their culture—labeling him or her a *Zhongguo tong*, an affectionate term meaning "China hand"—there are limits to acceptance. No outsider is ever completely successful in an effort to be more Chinese than the Chinese.

Exactly how much the differences matter to the Chinese depends in part on the prevailing political situation in China. Even those Westerners who had lived in the PRC as Chinese citizens for decades following the 1949 revolution were ostracized during the Cultural Revolution, their foreignness suddenly making them suspect during that unfortunate period of rampant xenophobia.

Calls for a rejection of "bourgeois" influences and for a return to core socialist values have come at various intervals since China reopened its doors to the outside world in 1979, usually in the form of campaigns—against "spiritual pollution," against "peaceful evolutionism," and, most recently, in support of "spiritual civilization." Their timing and duration and the degree to which they are taken seriously are fairly reliable signals of which factions in the government happen to have the upper hand at any given time.

For example, the government's schizophrenia on this issue came out clearly with the launching and rapid abortion of the "anti–spiritual pollution campaign" in 1983. During this period one faction of government officials railed against corrupting influences stemming from China's opening to the West, and urged a return to conservative socialist values. Western music, dress, and values in general came under shrill attack. And some individuals who cultivated close relationships with foreigners were considered suspect. Before the campaign got very old, however, cooler heads prevailed and it was summarily abandoned by the government.

In the late 1990s, the climate has been one characterized by nationalism and jingoism, with foreign influences again blamed in some quarters for a degeneration of morals in China. The government has tried to promote a return to socialist values and Chinese "spiritual civilization." Foreign companies have been taken to task in the press for dominating the local marketplace and edging out local brands, as well as for producing substandard products for the local market. Where this will lead remains to be seen, but if it follows the trend of the past, it will probably fade in the next wave of liberalization.

As far as trying to be Chinese is concerned, many "China hands" have found that the best strategy is to glory in the cultural differences while minimizing the barriers. That is, they try to learn as much as they can about how the Chinese do things, and use this knowledge in their interactions with them. But they never lose sight of the fact that they are indeed different, and that this very distinction, even if it is sometimes a disadvantage, on balance confers considerable advantages on them when they interact with the Chinese.

BUSINESS RELATIONSHIPS

It is the business and professional relationships between Chinese and foreigners with which the PRC government feels most comfortable. After all, the principal justification for China's opening to the West has always been to acquire the technology and knowhow needed to fuel its modernization drive. The PRC's opening has never been driven by a strong sense that China can realize much benefit from the culture or social thought of foreigners. Thus it is professional relationships that the government recognizes and supports, not personal liaisons, though these are increasingly tolerated as well.

Business relationships generally begin rather formally. Informality is acceptable only after those involved have spent sufficient time together to know one another well, and even then it has its limits. In such situations, the Chinese don't always say what they mean or what they feel, but try instead to say and do what is proper and correct, or what will give them the most advantage. They deal with foreign businesspeople less as individuals and more as representatives of their organizations.

This is true even in the relatively informal social settings of banquets. While the Chinese work hard trying to establish common ground and interests—even personal interests—they never lose sight of the fact that the reason they are spending time with you is a professional one rather than a personal one. If you are also in business, chances are the same thing is true of you.

Rank is extremely important in business relationships with the Chinese. Even though it is sometimes hard to determine the rank of someone who comes from an entirely different system, still less to relate it to your own organizational hierarchy, the Chinese can be counted on to try their best at this. And as Chinese enterprises move farther away from the Soviet bureaucratic model and closer to the Western corporate model, signals get easier to read on both sides. It's unusual to talk business with someone who ranks far higher or far lower than you do, and if you find yourself in such a position, it's a safe bet that something is wrong somewhere.

On the other hand, you will frequently find yourself dealing with someone a step or two higher or lower. If it is an initial meeting, it may just be an accident that that person is present. Maybe the Chinese misjudged your rank and couldn't figure out how important you really are, and sent an important official because they didn't want to take the chance of offending you. It may also be a deliberate signal by the Chinese that they attach great importance to your company. If someone of somewhat lower stature is sent, it may be a misunderstanding, or it may be a signal that less importance is placed on you and your business.

When you have a great deal of contact with individuals in a Chinese organization—in joint venture situations, for example—it's natural for some of the formality to break down as people get to know one another better. For many democratic-minded Westerners, this is an invitation to abandon artificial distinctions and establish "buddy" relationships with the Chinese. While this approach can work—and work well—with Chinese of equal rank, it can spell disaster with those of higher or lower stature.

Whether you like it or not, it's important in business situations to keep rank distinctions squarely in mind. This is probably as true among Chinese in Taiwan and Hong Kong and elsewhere as it is among mainlanders, though the pecking orders are a bit different when they are not set down by the government, as they are in the PRC. You should behave politely in any case, but with Chinese who rank higher, you must be extra careful to be correct in behavior without appearing in any way presumptuous.

Bear in mind that they do not see themselves as your equals, at least as far as their positions go. Although it is a hallmark of Chinese etiquette that someone of higher rank never appears to be condescending in behavior toward someone of lower rank, that's really just form—not substance. If you're not number one in your organization, don't use the chance opportunity of a meeting with the head man on the Chinese side to try to establish *guanxi*; the attempt will probably backfire and you will appear ill bred and gauche for trying.

When you deal with those who rank lower than yourself, the same principles apply. Never do anything to give the impression you think yourself more important than the other person—that would be immodest and would earn you only contempt. The Chinese admire people who don't put on airs, but neither should you be overfriendly or too informal. Lower-ranking Chinese, especially less educated, less sophisticated, and more old-fashioned ones, want to be deferential to you. Knowing exactly where you fit in makes them comfortable. It's when you attempt to bridge the gap and deal as a peer or a friend that they become uneasy and uncertain how to behave.

Remember also that if you are a foreigner, for better or worse you are automatically considered to be someone worthy of some deference among many Chinese. There is a certain amount of rank—and privilege—that just goes with the territory. A Chinese factory manager may drop everything and give you a personal guided tour of his or her plant, or a Chinese store clerk may wait on you before a Chinese shopper who arrived before you did. However undeserving you may be of this extra bit of attention and solicitousness, it's better to accept it with grace and style—not as your due, but rather as the unselfish show of hospitality that it is—than to refuse it in protest. It's just one of the ways that the Chinese have of showing you that you are welcome.

A former colleague of mine reports a memorable experience that illustrates both how much regard the Chinese may hold for foreigners and how unaware we sometimes are of the turmoil we can cause when we are doing no more than being ourselves. She had been invited to give a talk to a Chinese unit about a business matter in which they were very interested. This was apparently one of the very few meetings where someone forgot to serve the obligatory tea, and as she talked on her throat became more and more parched, until she finally asked for a drink of water. Time passed, but no water ever came.

A few days later, my friend happened to run into the woman responsible for setting up the meeting. The hostess thanked her profusely for an excellent presentation, and added that she was sure my friend would be interested to know that a meeting had been held and the worker who had been responsible for providing liquid refreshments that day had been soundly criticized for dereliction of duty.

There's a word of warning in this tale: Be careful what you say to a senior-level official about work done by his or her staff. If you criticize the arrangements made for your trip, for example, *somebody* is going to hear about the mistakes after you've gone. Unless you are bound and determined to make heads roll, communicate criticism quietly on the staff level, not publicly to the boss.

FOREIGN WOMEN AND BUSINESS

The Chinese are generally fairly accepting of business relationships with foreign women, a major difference between them and their Japanese and Korean counterparts. Women are nominally equal in China, the mainland government maintaining that they were "liberated" along with men in 1949 when the PRC was founded. In actual fact, females in important government or business decision-making positions in China are really quite few, and proportionately not much different from the number one sees in the more developed societies of the West.

For Chinese on the mainland and elsewhere, the operative word in the term "foreign female" is more often "foreign" than "female." Foreign businesswomen receive the respect due their positions, and no less of it than would a male with the same status. A foreign woman's sex does not place her at much of a disadvantage when she deals with Chinese males. The same dynamics would apply to a foreign businessman dealing with a Chinese businesswoman. The best course is to keep things cordial, but always a bit formal.

It would be exceptionally rare for a Chinese male to make an overture to a foreign female business acquaintance that could possibly be construed as untoward—unless he was indeed pursuing a sexual relationship with her, or she gave him a signal that she was interested in one. Such situations, while not unknown, are nonetheless rare in the extreme.

Wives of foreign businessmen are welcomed by the Chinese to accompany their husbands on business trips to China. Traditionally, they are not present during business meetings and negotiations, but are enthusiastically hosted at social occasions such as receptions and banquets. A wife is considered to share the rank of her husband, as is evidenced by the fact that she may even be called by her husband's title—not his name—with the addition of the term *furen* (Madame). Wives thus generally receive comparable treatment in terms of protocol. Although foreign spouses are commonly seen as banquet guests, Chinese spouses seldom show up at social occasions in the PRC, unless they have a business reason to be present. This tends to be true in Taiwan and Hong Kong as well, though perhaps a bit less so.

The Chinese are comfortable with this double standard, and no foreign guest should ever have second thoughts about bringing a spouse along on a social occasion, provided the spouse has been explicitly invited to participate. When extending an invitation to a Chinese business associate, it is acceptable to invite the person's spouse along, especially if your own will be present. But don't ever press the issue. And when you are a guest, it's best not to inquire why a particular Chinese has not brought along a husband or wife.

PERSONAL RELATIONSHIPS

Left to their own devices, Chinese people will often go out of their way to befriend foreign guests in their midst. While sometimes the motivation is potential personal gain, more often this penchant for hospitality—arguably one of their most endearing qualities—stems from genuine altruistic curiosity about people who are different from them. It does take a certain amount of boldness to approach someone of another culture, however, and not everyone is comfortable being so forward. While it's not uncommon to run into people who are apparently indifferent to foreigners, it's still relatively rare to bump into someone who is actively hostile. Sometimes, especially in rural and far-flung areas, the hospitality foreigners receive is exceptionally warm and genuine.

Among Chinese in Hong Kong, Taiwan, and Singapore, where there are no restrictions on these types of associations, it is common to find people who deal every day with foreigners, and who even number some Westerners among their close friends. Many an American or European student of the Chinese language has made great progress living with a Chinese family, or in a dormitory with a Chinese roommate.

However, foreigners who live in Hong Kong, where few if any restrictions on cross-cultural friendships have existed for the past several decades, sometimes report that friendships with local Chinese paradoxically seem harder to establish and maintain there than in China or Taiwan. It's as though the close working relationships that many Hong Kong Chinese have with foreigners during the business day and the level of knowledge of foreigners they glean from imported television programs and films render them relatively incurious about cultural differences. On their own time, many would rather pursue friendships with other Chinese.

In the PRC, there have traditionally been risks—sometimes real, sometimes just perceived—associated with deepening relationships with foreigners, and as a result, even in the relatively open climate of the late 1990s, some Chinese remain circumspect about keeping foreign friends at arm's length. Even in less politically charged periods, foreign journalists and diplomats continue to be most carefully scrutinized. They are viewed in more paranoid Chinese circles as little better than spies. But as the number of foreigners resident in China grows, Chinese authorities have become less fearful of even these relationships. Many Chinese citizens are now forthcoming with foreigners of all stripes, and they seem far less concerned about potential risks than was the case a few years ago.

If you are interested in developing a personal relationship with a Chinese, it's best to follow his or her lead. By all means show your interest, but if you encounter any apprehension at all, it's best to back off and apply no pressure. Your Chinese friend is a better judge of whether any serious threat exists in his or her particular situation. If the friend seems unconcerned, there is probably little reason for excess caution.

A Chinese friend will view the requirements of friendship through his or her own lenses, however, and so in entering into a friendship with a Chinese, you must expect to be judged according to Chinese standards. Casual acquaintance does not demand any significant commitment among Chinese, but friendship implies obligation—obligation to drop everything and help out a friend in need, obligation to use connections and *guanxi* on behalf of a friend. Not to deliver puts you at risk of being labeled as insincere—a cardinal sin.

Even healthy personal relationships with the Chinese may sometimes strike Westerners as a bit too formal or correct for their taste. This behavior should not be misinterpreted as coldness; it is precisely because the Chinese party values the friendship that he or she will want to make sure that nothing goes wrong with it. Chinese sometimes say that Westerners are frequently overly polite to strangers and not solicitous enough of their friends; they themselves tend to err in the opposite direction. A Chinese doesn't feel it incumbent upon him or herself to be at all concerned about a stranger, but to be discourteous or disrespectful to a friend is a serious offense.

While it is thus a good idea to be circumspect when dealing with Chinese friends, this doesn't by any means imply that you must always be grave or serious. Kidding around can work well with the Chinese, just so long as the ground rules are made clear. This is not as easy as it sounds, however. Joking and jesting may not be understood at first, and it may take quite a while for Chinese friends or colleagues to get used to it. The good news is that once Chinese realize that all is in fun and that any barbs that come their way are not to be taken seriously, they often learn to play the game as well as any Westerner.

My own personal relationships with Chinese people have been most successful when they are honest and fairly frank. Because the cultural barriers offer so much opportunity for misreading signals, being less than candid can result in serious misunderstandings. Frank discussion of issues sometimes bears the risk of running afoul of the Chinese propensity for correct, cordial relations and surface harmony at all times. It is, however, a fairly effective precaution against any serious threat to the relationship posed by unspoken feelings that are allowed to fester when an action or a statement is read incorrectly. But the more candid the discussion, the more important it is to hold it in private. That way any potential face considerations are minimized.

Being Entertained in a Chinese Home

When the PRC opened to foreigners in the 1970s, they were virtually never invited to Chinese homes. Foreigners who traveled to China were always there on some sort of business, and business entertainment in China generally takes place in restaurants and hotels. There was never any call to entertain at home, a practice usually reserved for hosting very close friends. In the few cases in which such invitations were issued, the host had first to secure the approval of his or her work unit.

In this early period there was a real fear of being perceived by neighbors as deliberately trying to cultivate foreign friends for personal benefit—an offense that could lead to investigation by the public security authorities in the area. While these fears have by and large disappeared today, there can still be some hesitation about inviting a foreigner to one's home, since doing so can still cause a stir in some neighborhoods, and one of the lessons of recent PRC history is that being in the spotlight can lead to trouble.

Then too, many Chinese live in very modest and spartan settings, and those who do may be painfully conscious of the fact that they lack the amenities necessary to make foreign guests comfortable—hot running water, Western-style toilets, carpeted floors, or comfortable furniture, for example. Discharging social obligations through entertaining at restaurants is still the most common course in China.

The use of public places for entertainment—both business and personal—is common practice among Chinese in Hong Kong, Macao, Taiwan, and other Asian countries as well. Foreigners are frequently invited out to restaurants by Chinese people. These can be very pleasant occasions, though they can sometimes end in a battle over who pays the check. Splitting the bill was traditionally unheard-of among Chinese; one person is generally expected to take responsibility for the whole check, though young people are beginning to adopt this Western practice.

In any event, if it has been made very clear up front who is host and who is guest, then there will be relatively little disagreement when the time comes to settle the bill; the guest may make a gesture toward paying, but the host will generally prevail. If it is unclear, however, there may be a considerable amount of back-and-forth before agreement is reached, since face is at stake.

Unless it has been made clear at the outset that your counterpart is the host for the meal, it is polite to offer to pay, but sometimes it is not polite to prevail. And it is often hard to know if a Chinese really wishes to treat or is just being polite. If you are unclear on this point, think back to who "owes" whom in the grand scheme of things, that is, who invited whom out last, who did a favor for whom most recently, and so on. And think back to who suggested the meal in the first place. But note also that if you are visiting a Chinese friend or business contact and are on his or her home turf, the assumption is generally that your counterpart will pick up the check, not you. Similarly, when you are in your home country, you generally are the one who plays host.

The practice of inviting foreign friends over for a home-cooked dinner is growing in popularity in the PRC. It's often easier for a Chinese with whom you have absolutely no business connections to do this than one who may be in a position to negotiate with you at some point. But at any rate, it is no longer a rarity for a foreigner resident in China—or even a visitor with a number of Chinese friends—to receive such an invitation.

If you are asked to a Chinese home, the visit will almost always revolve around the taking of a meal. To offer less would be to fail as a host according to Chinese standards. When the invitation is first extended you may receive a mixed message: Although you will be warmly welcomed, and your host really wants you to accept, he or she may offer apologies for the rudimentary nature of the facilities. It's proper in this situation to do what will probably come naturally: Reassure the host that wherever he or she lives and whatever has been planned will be fine with you.

If you must decline the invitation for some reason, by all means explain what the conflict is. If you don't take the trouble to do this, the Chinese will read your response as a rebuff, and will assume that your real reason for declining is that you do not wish to pursue the relationship with him or her. Since this constitutes something of a loss of face, you will likely not be asked again, and it's possible that you may notice an unpleasant change in your relationship with the person. It's thus best not only to give a concrete excuse, but also to make it clear that you would be pleased to accept an invitation for another time.

If you accept the invitation, it's best to inform the host if you have any dietary restrictions or idiosyncrasies, for either health or religious reasons. You might do this in any country; it makes good sense and it heads off misunderstandings later. When you arrive, do bring a gift with you. If you know the person well, bring something you think he or she might like. If you don't, a carton of foreign cigarettes, a bottle of imported liquor or wine, a basket of tropical fruit, or a box of foreign-made chocolates are good, all-around gifts that are usually very much appreciated. Avoid cut flowers, as the Chinese associate these with funerals. If the gift is wrapped, the host may not open it in front of you unless you specifically request it (see Chapter 9). If you have selected the gift carefully and wish to be present when it is opened, explain to the host that you hope he or she will follow the Western custom of opening the gift in front of the giver. But don't insist if you encounter any resistance.

The preliminaries—tea and conversation in a sitting area—will probably resemble those of a formal banquet held at a restaurant (see Chapter 8). Never ask for food or drink; it's polite to wait until it is offered. Don't be put off by the fact that the hospitality may seem excessively formal to you—again, the correctness probably only reflects the value placed on the relationship. As the meal proceeds, you will probably notice that the emphasis on protocol will wane, until it feels more and more like an informal gathering of friends.

In most Chinese households, it is the mother who is responsible for cooking, though there are exceptions. She is likely to greet you when you first arrive, and then disappear into the kitchen to cook the dinner. Since Chinese meals are generally served a course at a time, and since most Chinese live in one-wok homes, the mother may not reappear until she has churned out all of the dishes. She will then eat what is left. In such situations it is not necessary to wait until the cook is finished before eating; indeed, to do so will only make the host nervous and uncomfortable. It's gracious to ask after the mother and to wonder aloud if she will be joining in the feast, but by all means follow the host's lead and eat when the food is first served. Eat a lot to show that you are enjoying the food. But don't eat the last bit of any dish; leave a taste for the cook. If you finish every last bit of food it's an indication that the host has not prepared enough.

Be sure to find nice things to say about the surroundings and the food. Relentlessly counter every apology you hear (for example, "The food is really not so tasty," or "My wife is not such a good cook") with a protest and a compliment. After the meal is over, wait a respectable period of time before leaving. If you rise to leave too abruptly, your host may conclude that you have been offended in some way. Since Chinese by and large are early diners, dinner may be over as early as eight thirty in the evening. On the other hand, don't stay late into the night; it is a good rule of thumb to leave between a half hour and an hour after the meal is finished.

It's good manners to repay the invitation if this is possible, though this courtesy is not strictly required. If, for example, you are just passing through and will not have enough time in the city to host a return meal, you are relieved of the obligation. Even if you do reciprocate, it need not be in kind; you may invite the host's family on an outing, a picnic, or a meal in a restaurant.

DRESS

It used to be a faux pas to present a tie clip as a business gift to someone in the PRC—an absurdity in the land of the Mao jacket, where ties were nowhere to be seen. Yet some of the most obvious changes in China during the 1980s have occurred in the area of acceptable forms of dress. Western clothing is now the rule rather than the exception, and to give the occasional tie tack or even a pair of cufflinks isn't necessarily such a bad idea anymore.

Dress in the People's Republic of China until the 1980s was a dreary affair. There was little choice; men were expected to wear Mao jackets—loose-fitting jackets actually called *Zhongshan zhuang* by the Chinese, after the Mandarin pronunciation of the name of Sun Yat-sen, the father of modern China and the man who first made them popular. They were available in blue, brown, green, and gray—period. Loose-fitting white shirts were the rule, worn tucked at the waist under sweaters in cold weather, or hanging out over the belt in the summer.

For women, a pantsuit variation on *Zhongshan zhuang* with an open-collared tunic and a pair of slacks was standard. There were no skirts or dresses, and even the traditional Chinese dress, the *qipao*, a tight-fitting garment with a high collar and a long slit up the leg, was forbidden as bourgeois and too revealing. The few colors that were available were dark and conservative. Only children were permitted to dress in bold, festive colors. The bright reds, blues, and oranges visible in any kindergarten class gave one the distinct impression that people were enjoying these forbidden colors and styles in the only way they could—vicariously through their children.

This was the era in which communist China was derided abroad as a "nation of blue ants." And indeed, some customs regarding dress were fairly regimented—such as the official switching over to the summer uniform that occurs nearly universally on May 1 whether the weather has changed or not. This practice continues to this day, in fact, among uniformed government employees.

Standardization of dress probably got its start as the dictum of a government committed to stamping out individualism, but in later years it became more a function of social pressure than anything else. The Chinese take much comfort in conformity. It's when you are obviously different from others that you turn yourself into a lightning rod for criticism and shame. A Chinese expression says it all: *Qiang da chutou niao*. It means "The gun shoots the bird that sticks its head out."

Most of this is now safely in the past. Western dress is the rule in China today, and one seldom sees the Mao suit except among the very old, the very poor, or the state leader who occasionally wants to make a political point—as President Jiang Zemin did when he appeared in *Zhongshan zhuang* at the White House during his 1997 state visit. Skirts and dresses are now worn by women more frequently than are the Chinese-style pantsuits described above. Bright colors are worn by adults. And even makeup, once roundly criticized as bourgeois, is now quite common, especially among city dwellers.

Because many offices and meeting rooms on the mainland are unheated, it's a good idea to dress warmly during the winter months if you expect to spend much time meeting with government or state-owned enterprises. To cope with this problem, the Chinese generally dress in layers—long underwear, a shirt, a sweater, a bulky tunic, and a winter coat. It's a simple matter to peel off a layer or two should the surroundings get too warm.

It is not an overgeneralization to say that as a rule, Chinese on the mainland don't care at all how foreigners dress, unless of course they wear clothing that offends the Chinese sense of propriety. As long as you stay with reasonably conservative garments, this should not be much of a problem. Women should avoid clothing that is too revealing, such as tight tank tops, halter tops, see-through blouses, and excessively short skirts.

Short pants on foreigners have traditionally evoked stares, though this is changing somewhat as they grow in popularity among the Chinese themselves. Still, if you have exceptionally hairy legs, count on raising an eyebrow or two on the streets of most Chinese cities if you opt to wear shorts.

Provided your clothing is not too revealing, the Chinese will not be sensitive to what you wear. Don't bother asking them what the appropriate dress is for a particular event; they will probably only suggest that you wear what makes you comfortable. A sweater and skirt will generally do as well as a dress, and a jacket and tie can generally fill in for a suit. For important occasions like a banquet in Beijing's Great Hall of the People, you will certainly want to dress well, if only because the other foreign guests who attend will probably be decked out. But a dark suit is as formal as China gets for men; only in rare events sponsored by foreigners will you ever have a need for a tuxedo, and even then, it's usually optional.

RECAP: NINE TIPS FOR FOREIGNERS IN CHINA

1. The Chinese are generally extremely hospitable and quite pleasant to Western visitors. Their view of the West is often schizophrenic, however: Westerners seem highly advanced in many ways, but lacking in morals at the same time.
2. In the absence of another set of standards, many Chinese judge Westerners and their behavior according to their own norms. But expectations are low. Displaying some knowledge of Chinese customs earns you admiration.
3. Business relationships generally begin formally. Rank distinctions are important; with those of higher station you must be careful to be correct in behavior and not to appear presumptuous.
4. When dealing with a lower-ranking person, never give the impression that you think yourself more important than the other person, but don't be too informal, either.
5. The Chinese accord foreign businesswomen all the respect due their positions. Spouses of foreign businessmen are welcomed by the Chinese at social occasions. A wife

is considered to share the rank of her husband and vice versa. Chinese spouses seldom show up at social occasions on the mainland, however.

6. Chinese may be circumspect about keeping foreigners at arm's length, though this is changing quickly. Casual acquaintance does not demand any significant commitment, but friendship implies obligation to the Chinese.
7. If you are asked to a Chinese home, the visit generally includes a meal. If you must decline, explain what the conflict is; if you don't, the Chinese will read your response as a rebuff.
8. If you accept, bring a gift with you. Eat a lot to show that you are enjoying the food. Counter every apology you hear with a compliment. After the meal, wait a respectable period of time before leaving. And reciprocate the invitation if possible.
9. Western dress is growing in popularity in the PRC, but the Chinese remain uncomfortable with clothing that is very revealing. The Chinese are not otherwise particularly sensitive to what foreigners wear, so wear what makes you comfortable. Formal dress is seldom if ever necessary in the PRC.

Chapter VIII

The Chinese Banquet

A COLLEAGUE OF MINE WHO WAS WALKING DOWN A STREET IN Beijing once happened to run into a Chinese government official whom he had escorted around the United States on a delegation trip earlier that year. The Chinese was delighted to see him, and asserted immediately that the vice minister who had headed that delegation would be happy to learn that my co-worker was in town and would insist on inviting him out to a banquet.

The Chinese being magnanimous hosts, they invited me to go along as well. But when we arrived at the restaurant at the appointed time, it was apparent in short order that the vice minister, who was at that point on the verge of retirement, didn't really remember my colleague at all, and in fact only had a dim recollection of his trip to the United States. But that didn't really make much difference. Though the conversation was somewhat labored, the food was excellent, and everyone had a good time.

I learned two lessons from this experience. First, foreigners are not necessarily invited to Chinese banquets because of any strong personal bonds. The feasts are principally used by the Chinese as vehicles to deliver on social obligations—in this case, a way to say thanks for the hospitality the Chinese group had received some months before in the United States. The second lesson was that banquets aren't necessarily held for the benefit of the guest. Often the guest simply provides a convenient excuse for Chinese workers to partake of a good meal at someone else's expense, or to deliver on obligations to fellow Chinese who can be invited to the same banquet.

This isn't to say that there aren't often very warm feelings between hosts and guests at banquets, especially when they have shared experiences—such as a trip down the Yangzi River or days of protracted contract negotiations. It is simply to point out that among the Chinese, banquets serve many purposes in addition to sampling good food and drink.

ENTERTAINING OUT

It is relatively unusual for Chinese to entertain foreigners in their homes; they may be embarrassed about their modest living conditions compared to those of the outside world, or they may simply not have enough room to accommodate a full complement of dinner guests. Playing host to a guest at a meal in a nice restaurant has always been a practical solution; it is common practice in China as well as elsewhere in Asia.

Among the Chinese, there are a thousand excuses for holding a banquet: to welcome or say farewell to a visiting delegation from a foreign country; to mark the signing of a business agreement; to reciprocate for a banquet held in one's own honor on a different occasion; to celebrate a birth, a wedding, or a relative's sixtieth birthday; to observe the Spring Festival, Mid-Autumn Festival, or some other holiday; to show appreciation for a kindness or a favor; to send a friend off on a long trip or to welcome one back. Banquets vary in formality depending on the nature and importance of the occasion, the number of people, the location, the individual personalities involved and their relationships with one another.

Banquets have become so commonplace, in fact, that from time to time the government has cracked down on some of the excesses associated with them. Specific government organizations and state-owned enterprises have been criticized for spending too much money on them. Municipal governments have ordered bureaus under their aegis to keep the number of formal meals to a minimum and to keep expenditures on such entertainment to reasonable levels. But because of their importance in keeping the "balance of favors" more or less in equilibrium and their ability to confer face on both the host and guest, banquets have never been in much danger of extinction in China.

The Formal Banquet

In formal banquets, guests receive invitation cards prior to the occasion that officially request their attendance. The cards are often mere formalities, issued only after the host knows the guest has agreed to attend. An intermediary has usually made contact and determined whether the time is convenient. The cards specify date, time, and place and name the host, often using fairly honorific language (for example, "Please grace us with your honorable presence").

Invitations are generally written in Chinese or in both Chinese and English. They may include a request for an R.S.V.P. They are often hand-delivered, and may arrive as late as a few hours before the meal is scheduled to begin, though generally only after a verbal invitation has been proffered and accepted. Only at large, formal gatherings in locations such as Beijing's Great Hall of the People or Diaoyutai State Guest House must invitations actually be produced in order for guests to gain entry into the banquet hall.

If the banquet is being held in honor of a delegation, the members of the group are expected to arrive together. This avoids any awkwardness that could ensue if an important guest were late, but others arrived on time. Promptness is considered a virtue among the Chinese, and it is never polite to keep a host waiting, still less a guest. It is proper for the hosts to arrive at the restaurant early and to be in the banquet room waiting when the guests appear. As with business meetings, the host typically stations a representative outside the door of the restaurant to escort the visitors to the banquet room upon arrival.

RECEPTION OF GUESTS

Chinese banquet rooms typically include groupings of comfortable, overstuffed chairs immediately adjacent to the dining tables. As a guest, you will be received in these seating areas when you arrive, unless the gathering is too large; in such cases only the principal guests will be so received. As in business meetings, if you are the principal guest you will be seated to the right of the principal host, with an interpreter stationed nearby to facilitate conversation. The second-ranking person in your party should be placed to the left of the host or somewhere else nearby and within earshot.

Tea is served, either by restaurant attendants or by someone in the host's party. Damp cloths are often provided as well for all to clean their hands and wipe their faces; they are provided piping hot in winter and cold in the summer, and are very refreshing. They may be left on a table or returned to a service person after use.

Conversation during this initial reception period, which generally lasts only about five minutes, is normally kept light and nonsubstantive. Your Chinese host may inquire about the details of your day, ask how you are enjoying your visit to China, or observe that you have managed to bring good weather along with you. After a signal from the restaurant staff that all is ready, the host will suggest that the group adjourn to the tables to begin the meal. He or she may say something like *Bian chi, bian shuo,* which basically means "Let's continue the conversation as we eat."

SEATING

When the host announces that it is time to sit down, all members of the host party help the guests find their seats, a polite gesture. Cards at each place setting declare who is to sit where. They are often written in the native language of the diner, a practice that helps you to find your own place but does not give much help in figuring out the name of the person seated at either side. When prepared properly, name cards are written in both languages. They may be placed at all of the tables or simply placed at the head table. In the latter case, those not seated at the head table may sit where they wish.

Seating at formal banquets is determined before guests arrive and is arranged according to fairly rigid protocol. It is not uncommon for the Chinese to change the seating plan a number of times before the event as R.S.V.P.s are received, and there is sometimes a flurry of activity at the last minute when a high-ranking person who was supposed to attend fails to show up. High-level guests must be accorded all of the respect and honor that their ranks dictate—failure to do this is considered an unpardonable faux pas—and everyone moves up a notch when someone of higher station does not appear.

Knowing who outranks whom is key to making proper seating arrangements. An ostensibly egalitarian society, the PRC is in fact exceptionally protocol-conscious. As a result, if the Chinese are not properly informed, they will make assumptions that are not necessarily accurate. When Chinese travel abroad, any delegation list they produce can be relied on to be an accurate indication of the relative rank of each of the members—people are listed in strict protocol order, from the top down. This protocol is important to them, and it helps everyone to understand each person's proper place in the scheme of things.

They expect the same from foreign groups visiting China. A friend of mine recalls a banquet several years ago in which seating assignments mysteriously appeared to have been made completely at random. Only after inquiries were made did it become clear that the cause was a simple alphabetical list of delegation members that had found its way into the hands of the Chinese hosts. Even today, anomalies still occur when the Chinese are not adequately informed. They find it as difficult to divine whether a senior vice president outranks an executive vice president in a given company as a foreigner might if he or she were trying to figure out whether a bureau chief is above a division director in a Chinese ministry.

The Chinese encourage foreign friends to bring their spouses to banquets if they have accompanied their husbands or wives to China, and in such cases invitations are usually extended explicitly to spouses. They seldom bring their own partners along, however, unless the relationships between host and guest are particularly close. When you host a banquet, it is polite to ask Chinese counterparts to bring their husbands or wives if you have spouses in your own party, but you should never push the matter if you are rebuffed—which you probably will be.

Banquets typically take place around round tables that seat between ten and twelve people each. As many tables will be arranged in the room as are necessary to seat all of the guests. The group should be distributed relatively evenly across all available tables so that a thirty-person banquet, for example, would most likely break down to ten people at each table rather than twelve, twelve, and six. If possible, the number of Chinese and foreigners should be in approximate balance at each table.

The table farthest from the door to the room is usually designated as the head table. The principal guest is seated there in a place of honor at the immediate right of the principal host, facing the door (or, if there is to be entertainment, facing the stage). An interpreter sits in the immediate vicinity, usually to the right of the guest, as shown in Figure 4.

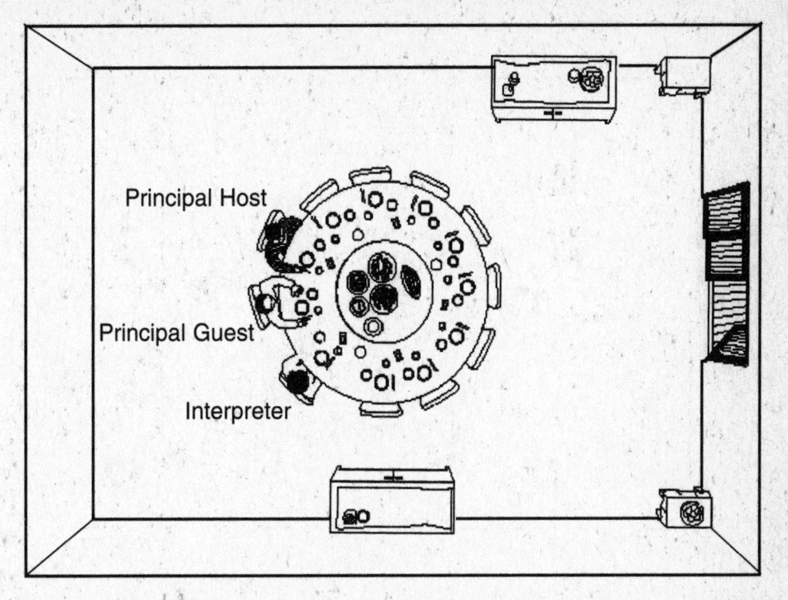

Figure 4. ***Seating of the principal host and guest.*** *The principal guest at a Chinese banquet sits facing the door to the room, to the immediate right of the principal host. An interpreter is stationed nearby to facilitate conversation.*

The second-ranking Chinese may sit directly across the head table from the principal host, with the second-ranking person in the guest party at his or her immediate right, just across from the principal guest. An interpreter is also placed in the immediate vicinity, as shown in Figure 5.

If this arrangement is used, the third- and fourth-ranking Chinese hosts and foreign guests are seated at the second table, fifth- and sixth-ranking at the third table, and so on, in a fashion similar to the head table, taking care that the main hosts at each table can maintain eye contact with the principal host.

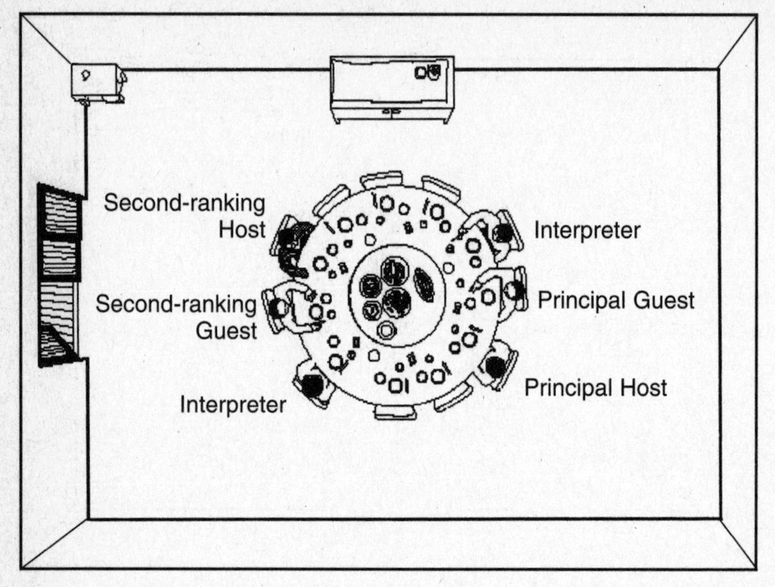

Figure 5. ***Seating of the second-ranking host and guest.*** *The second-ranking host is seated directly opposite the principal host, with the second-ranking guest immediately to his or her right.*

Alternatively, the second-ranking Chinese may be seated at the second table, with the second-ranking foreigner at his or her immediate right, mirroring the arrangement at the head table. The angle is shifted somewhat, however, again allowing the hosts to maintain eye contact, as shown in Figure 6.

Following this scheme, a third-ranking host and guest would be seated at table three, and so on until all available tables were filled. The next host in the hierarchy would fill in the second position at table one, then table two, and so on. In either scenario, lower-ranking guests are placed in empty seats until all tables are complete.

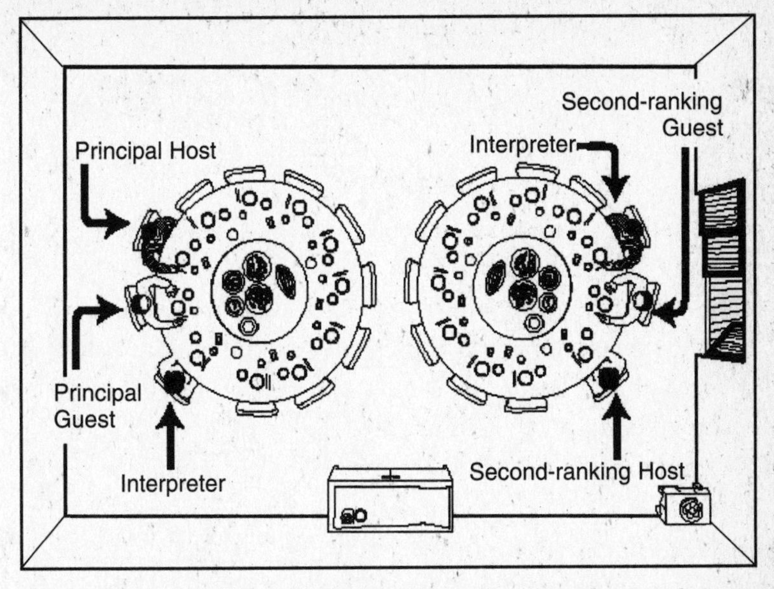

Figure 6. ***Alternative seating of the second-ranking host and guest.*** *Alternatively, the second-ranking host may be seated at a second table, with the second-ranking guest to his or her right. The angle is rotated a bit so that hosts may maintain eye contact during the meal.*

In China, round tables are the rule, and in my view they do a far better job of encouraging group interaction than do the rectangular tables popular in the West. Chinese protocol seating can be adapted to rectangular tables, however, if necessary. The same rules apply, except that the host is placed not at the short end of the table, but rather in the middle of one of the long sides of the rectangle, with the guest at his or her right. The interpreter may be seated across the table from them or to their left or right. In general, however, oblong tables do not lend themselves to Chinese-style banquets, and round tables are preferable.

Banquets often involve guests from organizations other than those of the hosts and the guests. A Chinese business executive or government official may invite a representative of another Chinese organization to a banquet for a foreign visitor, or perhaps more than one foreign company has sent delegates to China for a particular purpose, and the Chinese host is entertaining all of them together.

In such cases, the rule is that the senior individual from *every* major organization represented at the banquet should be accorded a place of honor, and this generally implies being seated at the head table, unless the person is too low-ranking for this to be appropriate. The place to the immediate left of the principal host is often used for such guests. Spouses of invited guests are accommodated at the same table as their partners unless this is not feasible (for example, if there are too many VIPs present, and including spouses at the head table would force some of them to move to table two). It is considered a special honor for a spouse to be placed in the seat immediately to the left of the host.

Common sense dictates that there be exceptions to any rigid seating protocol, and there are. For example, the Chinese find it as awkward as anyone else when people seated at the same table cannot communicate with one another because they have no common language. Thus interpreters are seated where they are needed, without regard to their rank and status. And other bilingual people, even if not officially designated as interpreters, are also dispersed as necessary.

THE PLACE SETTING

The basic place setting at a formal Chinese banquet consists of a bowl for rice or soup, a shallow dish for main courses, a smaller dish for condiments and sauces, a dessert dish, a porcelain spoon, a pair of chopsticks, and a porcelain chopstick rest (or else a metal rest for both chopsticks and serving spoon). There may be as many as three drinking glasses: a medium-sized glass for beer, soda, or juice; a smaller wineglass; and a piece of stemware reserved for hard liquor that is smaller still.

Not all the utensils need be present at all times; some are changed frequently after a course or two has been served. A lazy Susan—a circular rotating tray—sits in the middle of the table; entrees are placed on it, and individuals may rotate it at will in order to reach a dish. In China, everyone shares the entrees; you don't appropriate a dish for yourself, but rather you are served, family-style, from a common plate.

Visitors to China should endeavor to learn to use chopsticks if at all possible, if only because they may run into situations in which forks are nowhere in sight. The Chinese are not offended when one has not mastered the art of using chopsticks, but they do appreciate the effort. It isn't as hard as it may appear. When all else fails, the porcelain spoon may be used to scoop up food. It's a bit inelegant, but no serious breach of etiquette. And serving staff at most of the better restaurants in China today can find you a fork if you ask for one.

You'll seldom see a knife at a Chinese table. They are occasionally provided at the end of the meal for the purpose of peeling a piece of fruit, but they are not part of the standard table setting unless the meal is intended to be some kind of blend of East and West. The Chinese don't use knives while dining because they have traditionally considered the knife a weapon with no place at a table where friends are sharing a meal. Also, since cutting and chopping are both part of the Chinese chef's craft, they are typically done in the kitchen before Chinese food is cooked.

The Meal

A plate of cold—or rather, room-temperature—appetizers is generally on the table when the party first sits down, or else is served very shortly thereafter. There are usually at least four different delicacies, and there may be many more; sometimes they are served on several small plates arranged at the edge of the lazy Susan. To the Chinese, the presentation of food is as important as its taste, and nowhere is this more evident than in the cold platter, which begins the meal. The appetizers may be artfully arranged in the shape of a flower, a dragon, a goldfish, a peacock, a phoenix, a Chinese lantern, or a butterfly, to name just a few examples. And they may be made out of barbecued beef, duck, chicken, ham, pickled vegetables, bean curd, jellyfish, cuttlefish, seaweed, or any of a couple of dozen other ingredients.

When the table is laid, the place settings for the principal and second hosts at each table are augmented with an additional set of chopsticks, and perhaps an extra serving spoon. These implements are not used to eat, only to serve. This is as much a sanitary measure as it is a point of etiquette. The rule is that no one samples any dish until the principal host has broken into it first. He or she will serve the principal guest first and then any other guests within reach. Following this—or, sometimes, simultaneously—the second host does the same. Frequently the restaurant's serving staff takes over from there, dividing the remaining food among all the guests.

Only after a dish has been started in this way and the guests have been served may individuals freely help themselves to more. The banquet begins without fanfare when the host breaks into the cold platter. No grace or equivalent is said, nor are any other rituals observed. The host may say something like *qing yong*—literally, "Please use," but actually "Help yourself"—or may simply signal by example that it is time to start.

A fundamental rule of traditional Chinese banqueting is that it is the responsibility of the host and his or her party to make sure all guests are served. This obligation continues throughout the meal, and will find its expression in constant monitoring of the guest's plate. When the plate is empty, someone from the Chinese side will reach over to fill it—and without checking to see if the chosen morsel meets with approval. If you continue to clean your plate, someone nearby will continue to serve you food. Thus it is vitally important to *leave a small amount of food in your dish* when you have finished eating; this is the only clear signal you can give that you are not hungry for more.

Although the host party is theoretically responsible for feeding the guests, there is no rule that says a polite guest can't try to turn the tables. In point of fact, the Chinese will attempt to serve foreign guests at Chinese-style banquets whether they are technically the guests or the hosts, and whether the meals take place in China or abroad. If you, as a guest, attempt to return the compliment by reaching to fill the plate of a Chinese host, you may get a good-natured protest—in the form of *Buyao keqi*, or "You needn't be so polite,"—but it is nonetheless seen as a very well-mannered and even somewhat flattering gesture. If you don't have access to the special pair of serving chopsticks laid out for the hosts, however, you should take your own chopsticks and *reverse them*, serving others with the larger ends, opposite those that have gone into your mouth. This precaution serves the gods of both etiquette and hygiene.

From beginning to end, a banquet may have a dozen or more courses. Glance at the menu that is often placed on the table; even if it is written entirely in Chinese, counting the number of lines will give you a rough idea of what is in store and will help you pace yourself accordingly. Or you can ask a Chinese dinner companion to translate it for you. A common mistake is to eat heartily of the first few dishes and have no appetite left for what follows. This not only prevents you from enjoying some of the best entrees; it also may sometimes be misinterpreted by your hosts. If, in the middle of a banquet, you appear abruptly to lose interest in eating, it is possible that they may mistakenly conclude that they have done something to upset you.

After the cold platter come two to four stir-fried dishes, followed by a soup and then three or four larger, hot dishes that are considered the main courses. Look for considerable variety in ingredients, methods of preparation, and tastes in these courses. Likely as not there will be some red meat, some poultry, some fish, and some vegetables; something steamed, something roasted, something stewed, and something deep-fried; and something sweet, salty, sour, and spicy. Soups are not served at this stage; sweets may occasionally be served between courses to cleanse the palate.

The signal that the meal is coming to an end is usually the presentation of a whole fish, the last of the main courses. This is sometimes followed by a starch, either rice—a symbolic gesture, since people are seldom hungry for it at this point—or noodles or buns. Finally there is a sweet soup and a dessert, often fresh fruit of some kind.

The ingredients in most of the dishes are self-evident, but it's appropriate to ask what you are eating if you don't know. The Chinese love talking about food, and given half a chance they will be glad to give you a discourse on regional variations in Chinese cuisine. A word of warning, though: Some fancy banquet dishes have poetic names that give no information about their actual ingredients, such as "stuffed fairy feet with shrimp" (duck feet filled with ham, peas, and shrimp paste) "eight treasures rice" pudding (glutinous rice with lotus seeds, dates, peanuts, lychees, walnuts, raisins, candied orange peel, and red bean paste, or some variation of these) and "ants climbing up a tree" (ground pork served on a bed of rice vermicelli).

It is good manners to taste a bit of each dish that is served, especially if you are eating in someone's home. But if you absolutely cannot steel yourself to down a rubbery piece of sea slug, a chunk of dog meat, or a translucent green thousand-year-old egg, declining is certainly a better alternative than gagging at the table. Or learn to take a bit of the offending dish on your plate and push it around a bit so it looks as if you have sampled it, smiling politely when you decline additional servings. No one is likely to remember how much you served yourself, still less to criticize you for eating too little. And try to remember this feeling when a Chinese visiting your country politely abstains from the raw cauliflower in blue cheese dip you have so carefully prepared (see Chapter 13).

Conversation

There are no set rules concerning what may or may not be discussed in a banquet situation, except to let good common sense be your guide. Even if a delegation is in China for lengthy and complicated negotiations, the Chinese will not necessarily choose to continue those discussions over a meal. They may try to use the time to get to know their counterparts a little better and break the tension by engaging in some light-hearted conversation and fun.

There is no reason, however, that substantive conversation can't take place during a meal, provided that the exchange remains cordial and face is preserved at all times. Sometimes the principal host at a banquet is not a member of the negotiating team, but rather an official of very high rank with an interest in, or oversight over, the particular project or issue under discussion. The banquet may provide the only opportunity the foreign delegation gets to meet with this official, and to limit the conversation to simple pleasantries would be a waste of everyone's time. One caveat, though: Under no circumstances should the principal host be put in a position of having to refuse a request made by a member of the delegation. This constitutes a serious breach of etiquette (see Chapter 5).

When people on both sides already know one another reasonably well, conversation generally flows freely, since there are shared experiences to discuss. When this is not true there can be some awkward moments. While it is not necessary to fill every moment with witty conversation, prolonged silences are to be avoided if only because they make many people uncomfortable. Cross-cultural small talk can be hard to sustain over a period that may last for a few hours, but do make every effort.

Fail-safe topics of conversation that can come to the rescue include weather; Chinese food, geography, or language; your own history of travel in China or elsewhere in the world; your Chinese counterpart's travels abroad or your business reasons for visiting China. Even international politics can be discussed, as long as the discussion does not get heated. Chinese seldom stray from the official government position on geopolitical issues, and are even less likely to do so in a public situation. So as long as you don't expect to change anyone's way of thinking, as long as you feel you can conduct a dispassionate discussion on the topic, and as long as you don't mind a mini-lecture on China's point of view, it's perfectly all right to touch on Russo-Chinese relations, Hong Kong's history, the Cultural Revolution, or even—and this may surprise you—the future of Taiwan. Just be sensitive enough to steer the conversation elsewhere if you sense the mood stiffening at all.

Though the ostensible purpose of the banquet is for everyone to have a good meal and a good time, these situations—like any social situations—carry with them some obligations. For example, you are expected to keep a running conversation going with your counterpart on the other side. When Westerners find it difficult to identify common ground with their Chinese hosts or guests, they sometimes try to ameliorate the awkwardness by chatting in their native language with their own colleagues. Though it is perfectly acceptable to involve your teammate in a discussion, it is a real faux pas to give up trying to bridge the gap with the Chinese. Most often it isn't much of a trial at all, but if it is, keep trying anyway. Your effort will be appreciated.

Table Manners

There are certain differences between the Chinese and Western conceptions of appropriate table manners of which you should be aware. Most important, under most circumstances it isn't polite in China to touch your food—still less anyone else's food—with your hands. Chinese food is deliberately cut up into bite-sized pieces in the kitchen before it is served, so that chopsticks will be the only equipment necessary at the table.

Though the morsels of food are of manageable size, they may still contain bones or shells. The Chinese are fond of hacking through bone when cutting meat or poultry, or of leaving the shells on shrimp or other shellfish to preserve their flavor. You may see Chinese discard bones or shells on the table next to their place settings or even on the floor. This is not the finest of manners, but it is often done, especially on less formal occasions. At banquets you should remove bits of bone from your mouth (with chopsticks if possible) and place them in a small dish that is part of your place setting and is frequently removed by service personnel. Occasionally a bowl will be passed around for the express purpose of discarding these pieces.

Some of the finer points of Western table etiquette are unknown in China. It is not impolite to place your elbows on the table, for example. Nor do you need to wait until everyone has been served before you begin eating any particular dish. Dishes are not, as a rule, passed around the table; they are placed in the center and you reach across the table to get at them, even if you need to stand up to do so. You needn't worry about keeping your napkin in your lap. And service personnel are as likely to serve from the left as the right; there is no rule in China.

There is also no particular taboo against being a noisy eater. Don't be shocked if your host continues to talk through a mouthful of food, slurps his or her soup, belches, coughs, hiccups, or sneezes rather loudly during the meal.

It is seldom polite to handle food; always try to use an implement—chopsticks or a porcelain spoon. Unlike in the West, where it is considered acceptable to pick up a piece of chicken in your fingers, in China you endeavor to separate the edible from the inedible in your mouth if possible. There are, however, some circumstances under which Chinese do use their fingers: when consuming large steamed buns, animal joints and wings, or shellfish and whole, fresh fruit, for example. Just keep an eye on what your hosts are doing and follow suit, and you won't ever go far wrong.

When you are helping yourself at a Chinese banquet, use your eyes before you move your hand. That is, select the food you wish to retrieve in advance and then reach directly for it with chopsticks. What is to be avoided here is picking and poking through a common dish to find a chosen morsel. Also, try not to use the chopsticks to spear your food. This is no sin, but the Chinese don't do it. Try if at all possible to capture your food between the tips of two chopsticks.

If you should happen to drop a piece of food on the floor or the table, don't pick it up; just leave it there. If you drop a chopstick, pick it up and give it to a service person, who will replace it. If you pause during the meal, rest the tips of the chopsticks on the chopstick rests provided as part of the place setting. If these are not present, rest them on the rim of a dish; if only for sanitary reasons, they should not touch the table. Nor should chopsticks ever be stuck straight up into a bowl of rice when not in use; this reminds the Chinese of sticks of incense burned to pay homage to the dead. And you should never point at something with chopsticks.

Toothpicks are generally provided at the end of the meal. Feel free to use them, but be sure to cover your mouth with your free hand while you do so that your teeth are not visible to other guests.

Drinking and Toasting

Drinking figures prominently in the art of Chinese banqueting, just as it does in Chinese literature and mythology. Banquet guests most often are served wine and spirits as well as a choice of beer, juice, or a soft drink.

Drinking begins officially when the principal host offers a toast to the entire group. No one should drink spirits before then. If it is a large group, the host will stand and address all of the guests; a podium and/or microphone may even be used. The toast will be relatively short—two to four minutes is par for the course—and may be anything from a series of platitudes to a well-crafted discourse pregnant with meaning and symbolism.

In matters of high-level statecraft it's often the case that there is more to a dinner toast than meets the ear, as it were.

China watchers in foreign governments have been known to pore over the remarks Chinese leaders deliver to visiting heads of state in order to divine that obscure nugget of meaning lurking in the ambiguity. But in business or in leisure, a toast is generally no more than a hearty welcome or, at its most formal, perhaps a statement of principles.

A few courses—or, in some cases, immediately—after the principal host offers the toast, it is the principal guest's turn to do the same. It is always good form to offer a return toast. The remarks should be no longer than those of the host, and generally speaking, words that seem to come from the heart tend to evoke the best results. Sharing hopes for the successful conclusion of some business or warm feelings about your counterparts is a tried-and-true path. Also well trodden—but safe—are toasts to friendship among the people gathered in the room and their respective countrymen, pledges of cooperation, testaments to the principles of "equality and mutual benefit," and offers of reciprocal hospitality when your counterparts visit your own country.

The toasting ritual is pretty much the same on both sides of the Taiwan Strait. A word of warning is in order, however. If you offer the toast on behalf of the visiting delegation, you should take extra care to avoid an all-too-common pitfall of calling the PRC by the wrong name. The official name of the country is The People's Republic of China. It is also acceptable to refer simply to China in a toast.

What is not tolerable, and is in fact particularly offensive to PRC Chinese, is any reference to "The Republic of China," the name still claimed by the Nationalist government on Taiwan. As far as the communists are concerned, the Republic ceased to exist in 1949 when they gained control of the mainland; to them, Taiwan has no national status of its own and is simply a province of the PRC with delusions of grandeur.

It is also not considered correct in the PRC to use the term "communist China," as this implies that there is more than one China, and any hint of what they term a "two-Chinas policy" is thoroughly anathema to just about any mainland Chinese. The term "Greater China," which is being used increasingly by foreigners, does not seem to offend most mainland Chinese but is nonetheless politically incorrect for similar reasons. Truth to tell, even the term "mainland China" can be taken incorrectly by some, but when the subject of cross-straits relations comes up, the Chinese themselves often use it for clarity's sake, as have I in this book.

Needless to say, the situation is different if you are offering a toast to an audience in Taiwan. There a mention of The Republic of China will generally be welcome, as it confers legitimacy on the government. But if it is a very public occasion, you'd be wise to remember that the PRC government reads the Taiwanese press. The safest course is simply to refer to Taiwan and leave it at that.

In large and convivial banquets, the principal host and guest sometimes leave the head table and walk around to all the other tables in the room, offering toasts to the guests at each one. This is a very polite gesture, and those sitting at the other tables are expected to rise and acknowledge the toast.

Prior to the toast, you typically say *ganbei*, a Chinese phrase that literally means "dry glass," and has the same effect as "bottoms-up" in English, though a slightly befuddled interpreter once was heard to translate it as "bottoms together" to the amusement of the English-speaking guests. All join in at this point, and proceed to empty their glasses of spirits or wine. After drinking, the cups are turned upside down to demonstrate that they contain no more liquid. Emptying them is a bit easier than it may sound, since the glasses provided for these beverages are really quite small and hold about as much fluid as, say, a shot glass.

On the other hand, consider for a minute the contents of the glass. The beverage of choice for toasting is often some form of *baijiu* (spirits). The most prominent member of this family is *Maotai*, a fiery, 106-proof wheat-and-sorghum-based liquor that can quite literally catch fire or remove paint. The ability to down a glass of *Maotai* or any of its cousins is considered somewhat macho by the Chinese, but it is not required. You may also toast with wine, beer, or a soft drink, even if the person offering the toast is drinking something stronger. If you begin the meal by drinking *baijiu* and then switch halfway through to something softer, simply explain with a smile that you've had enough alcohol, lest someone misconstrue your behavior as a signal that you have taken offense at something that was said or done during the meal.

There is an alternative to *ganbei* if you don't feel up to emptying the glass. You can say *suiyi*, which means "at will," or "as you please." This frees you to drink as much or as little as you wish. If you do not wish to drink alcohol at all, you may simply make this clear at the start of the meal. One effective way is to tell your hosts you are allergic to alcohol. If you are male and use another excuse, be prepared for some good-natured ribbing on the part of the Chinese, who may attempt to goad you into drinking. But rest assured that if you don't choose to drink, they can be counted on to forbear; many Chinese don't drink liquor, either.

Strictly speaking, it is not polite to pour a drink for yourself; someone else at the table, ideally of the host's party, should notice that your glass is empty and take the initiative. This is especially true when you drink tea. If no one seems to notice that your glass is dry, pick up the decanter and fill someone *else's* glass; this generally results in the same being done for you.

Among the Cantonese, natives of China's southeasternmost province who also constitute most of the population of the Hong Kong SAR, there is a custom of rapping your knuckles or fingertips on the table to say thanks to someone who is filling your teacup and to signal when you have had enough; when you stop tapping, the person knows to stop pouring. This is not common practice among Chinese elsewhere, however, and may or may not be understood, but it is gaining in popularity these days, as are many other Cantonese customs.

It is not considered polite to drink alone at a Chinese banquet. You really should not drink at all before the initial toast is offered, except for beer or a soft drink. After the return toast is finished, however, it's pretty much a free-for-all. Anyone may offer a toast, either to the entire table, or to one or two individuals present. If you're really thirsty but don't have any meaningful remarks on the tip of your tongue, simply catch the eye of someone else at the table and raise your glass in the person's direction. He or she will then join you in a drink. Or, if you wish, steal a sip of beer or a soft drink on your own. Just be sure you are toasting someone else when you imbibe harder spirits.

Concluding the Banquet

Chinese banquets tend to last no more than one and a half to two hours. Dinners usually begin early—generally at about six or six thirty—and so by around half past eight or nine at the very latest the meal is essentially over. Unlike the West, China has no tradition of lingering after the meal; after the dessert is served, the banquet is over. A final glass of tea may be offered, and a damp cloth may be presented. The Chinese host may then observe that you are probably tired after your long day, or you may seize the initiative and remark that it has been a delightful meal and thank the host on behalf of your group.

Occasionally, the host may simply rise suddenly to indicate the end of the meal. This tends to happen at large gatherings where there are many tables, and where other tables may lag slightly behind the head table. The protocol in this situation is to stop eating even if there is food remaining; the banquet is officially over and guests are obliged to depart.

It is good manners to indicate to the host during the last course that you have eaten your fill. The Chinese expression *chi bao le,* which means "eaten one's fill," is useful here.

The guests rise to leave and are escorted to the door of the room by the principal host; it is not necessary for him or her to see them to their cars, though a member of the host's party will probably accompany them that far. The host remains behind. The bill is settled with the restaurant only after the guests have departed; it is not considered in the best of taste to handle money in their presence.

KARAOKE

In the old days, the evening was over when dinner was over. There was no nightlife per se in early 1980s China; people simply went home and went to sleep after a banquet. This still happens when guests and hosts do not know one another well, or when the relationship is a very formal one. But today, the mainland boasts lots of forms of late-night entertainment, and the conclusion of the banquet may only mark the beginning of the second part of the evening.

Karaoke, a Japanese invention that provides a soundtrack background for would-be Barbra Streisands and Frank Sinatras, made its debut in the late 1980s and took the PRC by storm. Karaoke machines have found their way into bars, discos, and many private banquet rooms, so the postbanquet entertainment need not involve any change of venue.

With karaoke, which is Japanese for "empty orchestra," the postbanquet entertainment is *you*. Most establishments provide books with the titles of songs they have on compact discs, and you get to choose the ones you wish to sing. The better establishments feature songs in the Mandarin, Cantonese, and Taiwanese (Hokkien) dialects as well as English and Japanese, so there is generally something for everyone. You would have to have been comatose throughout the history of pop music over the last forty years not to recognize a few titles from most karaoke song lists.

The good news is that as long as you can follow the tune, you don't have to have memorized the words. These appear for your convenience on a video monitor in the room, superimposed over generally irrelevant video footage. However, the words have often been transcribed by nonnative speakers of English who do their best to reproduce the song lyrics faithfully, but who may not really understand all that they are hearing. The results can be hilarious.

The other piece of good news is that you do not have to be a particularly good singer in order to be a good karaoke guest. You will realize this when you listen to some of the other guests. Enthusiasm and honest effort more than make up for lack of rhythm or pitch.

Quality karaoke machines permit you to adjust the pitch of the song until you find a comfortable key, and they come with microphones to amplify the voice of the singer or singers. The only real rule is to make sure that everybody who *wants* to sing gets a few opportunities to do so, and that people who really do *not* want to sing are not embarrassed into doing so. And, of course, to applaud a good performance—or, for that matter, even a bad one.

In formal business entertainment situations, the party who hosted the meal also hosts the karaoke, which generally includes drinks as well as the rental of the room, or a per-song fee. If you are among friends, other arrangements are possible, and it is entirely appropriate to pay for the evening's entertainment if someone else bought dinner. When the bill is settled, the evening really *is* over, and it is time to go home. But one caveat: Karaoke can be ruinously expensive in China, depending on where one goes and how much drinking and singing one does. If it is you who are planning the evening, it's wise to check out the rates in advance.

HOSTING A BANQUET

While you should say thank you at the end of a banquet, no formal thank-you notes for meals are written in China, nor are you expected to make a follow-up phone call to express your gratitude. The way to show appreciation—unless the banquet was offered to reciprocate some other favor in the first place—is by returning the favor in kind. This is not expected when a visiting group is only staying in a given city for a short time, but it is good form otherwise to treat your Chinese hosts to a reciprocal feast if the opportunity arises.

If you are in the position of playing host, the first problem you face is whom to invite. If it's a reciprocal banquet, the choice should be pretty easy: Invite essentially the same people who hosted you in the first place. But if it is not, you need to decide who your "target" high-ranking guest is, and proceed accordingly.

In the West, it is considered an honor to be *invited* to a banquet (even if one does not attend), so a host errs on the side of including on the invitation list all appropriate senior-level people who might possibly come, lest offense inadvertently be given. In China, one confers face when one *attends* an event like a banquet, and in so doing one does not want to be upstaged. There is, therefore, an unwritten rule that only one senior-level government official shows up at a given event. This is because if more than one leader attends, there is a risk that he or she will not be accorded the principal place of honor, and that translates into a loss of face.

What this means on a practical level is that sending courtesy invitations to several senior leaders to attend the same banquet in the hopes that at least one will come is precisely the wrong strategy to use in China if your goal is to secure high-level attendance. Rather, you need to go after one senior leader and make sure that everyone else who is invited is of lower rank. If it turns out that the principal target is unavailable, you can always try someone else. After all, if you are doing your job properly, you are not sending out invitations before you have checked to see who is available and willing to accept. Invitations go out only after a guest list is reasonably confirmed, and are generally mere formalities.

As far as making arrangements is concerned, there are some details of which you should be aware. First, you need to make a reservation at a hotel or restaurant with a private banquet room if possible. In making arrangements, you specify the price per head—the *biaozhun*—you are willing to pay. The restaurant will often give a range of fees and corresponding menus from which to choose. Some negotiation can occur here. Any of the prices quoted will generally result in enough food for the party; after a point, adding to the *biaozhun* only means that more exotic ingredients will be used—the sign of a quality banquet—not that more food will be served.

The *biaozhun* fee does not include liquid refreshments, which are charged for according to the amount consumed. You will be asked what beverages you wish to offer, however. *Maotai* or one of its fiery cousins, a wine, beer, and a soft drink are traditional fare in very high-class banquets, but the spirits, which are sometimes fabulously expensive, can easily be omitted with no major consequences. In fact, French wines are fast gaining ground at *Maotai*'s expense in Beijing. You may also be asked if you wish cigarettes to be provided in the banquet room, though this happens less and less frequently as China has moved to discourage smoking in public places.

It's generally safe to leave the specifics of the menu to the discretion of the restaurateur; you'll seldom be disappointed with what you are served. If you have a particular dish in mind, however, don't hesitate to suggest it. And you may review the menu in advance and suggest changes if you so desire; if you know your party will dislike a certain dish, tell the restaurant to think of a substitute. Resist the desire to scratch the sea slug or the fish maw from the menu, however; as unappetizing as these entrees may be to foreigners, the Chinese relish them as delicacies. They also serve as tangible evidence that you haven't skimped on the price. While it may be poor manners in the West to be ostentatious in one's choice of dishes, in today's China conspicuous spending and consumption is, alas, de rigueur.

The restaurant's manager may also want to know who your Chinese guests will be. This is not necessarily idle curiosity; the manager may want to know how important your guests are in order to determine how hard the staff needs to work on the meal to preserve the face of the restaurant. He or she also may know the principal guest and want to be on hand personally to express a greeting when the person arrives at the restaurant.

You should also know that it is a Chinese custom to provide for the chauffeurs who bring attendees to the banquet. This does not mean that drivers take part in the meal itself; it simply means that a fee—considerably less than the per-head charge for your banquet—is often paid to the restaurant to feed them in a separate room. If you are the host, it is customary to provide for your own group's drivers as well as those of the guests. Recently, however, the custom has evolved into a direct cash payment to drivers, who may either eat at the restaurant—which is probably excessively expensive by their standards—or go to a less expensive establishment and pocket the difference. Regardless, the restaurant can take care of this detail and will bill you accordingly. The standard charge for this in Beijing in 1998 was 50 *renminbi*, or about $6.00.

When planning the banquet, draw up your guest list and check with the liaison from your Chinese host organization, if you have one, to see if you are asking the right people (for a discussion of host organizations, see Chapter 2). The principal guest should be of approximately equivalent rank to the head of your group, or else there may be some discomfort on the Chinese part. Use an intermediary if possible to sound out the guests; it isn't polite to put someone in the position of having to decline an invitation to your face. If someone cites a concrete time conflict when declining, he or she is probably sincere. If a vague excuse is given, however, chances are greater that the person just doesn't want to accept your hospitality.

Beware also of trying to invite very high-ranking people from more than one organization to the same banquet. This often raises serious protocol issues, as high-ranking people expect to be the guest of honor at banquets they attend, and according to Chinese seating protocol there can be no more than one principal guest at a banquet. This does not mean you can't invite people from different organizations; it means only that you have to be careful with high-ranking cadres. When in doubt, consult a Chinese friend or liaison, who will probably know instinctively what to do. A good source is usually the external affairs section of your host organization, or of the Chinese organization that will send the most senior person to the banquet.

When you are putting on the banquet, the host's responsibilities detailed above, for example, arranging name cards, seating the guests, making sure that plates are kept full, and toasting, all devolve upon you. Remember that even if you forget some of the finer points of Chinese etiquette, a good-faith effort to do things according to Hoyle will not be wasted on the Chinese. They will happily pitch in and make the banquet a pleasant experience.

Recap: The Ten Commandments of Banqueting

When You Are the Host

1. Make sure your guests are met at the door and escorted to the banquet room. Be present in the room before they arrive so that you can welcome them properly.
2. Pay close attention to protocol, and don't slight anyone by seating him or her inappropriately. If you are not sure exactly how high someone's rank is, be sure to ask. Following standard seating arrangements is always a good idea.
3. Lead your guests to the table and help them find their seats. Use place cards to designate assigned seats; these should be in both English and Chinese if possible.
4. Keep a sharp eye on your guests' plates and make sure they are kept full of food. As long as the guests keep cleaning their plates, keep serving them even if they protest.

When You Are the Guest

5. Always leave something over on your plate at the end of the meal. Not to do so implies that you are still hungry.
6. Try to sample every dish if you possibly can. It is not a cardinal sin to eschew a particular dish, however. Pace yourself; there are probably more dishes coming than you think. Count on about a dozen of them in a formal banquet.
7. Don't suddenly stop eating or drinking in the middle of a meal, lest you cause your Chinese counterparts to think they have offended you.

8. Decide in advance whether you will drink alcohol or not, and stick to it. Don't start out with *Maotai* and suddenly switch to Coca-Cola unless you explain that you've simply had enough alcohol.

Anytime

9. Never drink hard liquor alone; always find someone to drink with you. Whenever you are thirsty, however, it is all right to drink some beer or a soft drink.
10. Be a good sport and sing a song if you find yourself in a karaoke party. Enthusiasm counts for more than rhythm or pitch.

Chapter IX

Gift-Giving

THE CHINESE—INDEED, ASIANS OF JUST ABOUT EVERY stripe—are inveterate gift-givers. Gifts may be given as tokens of esteem or gratitude, as souvenirs, as gratuities, or as payoffs. They may also serve to discharge obligations or mark occasions, or they may accompany overt requests for favors or some other type of patronage. It's especially important for business travelers to be aware of when gifts are and are not expected, and what types of gifts are most appropriate. But even casual travelers should be prepared to offer gifts when the situation requires it.

BUSINESS GIFTS

Delegations visiting mainland China are generally expected to offer to those who host them some sort of token of their visit. Conversely, Chinese traveling to other countries are nearly always prepared with gifts for those who receive them. In the PRC, the modus operandi has traditionally been to present one large gift to the host organization as a whole rather than a number of small gifts to its individual members. This approach sidestepped an issue peculiar to a socialist system, that is, whether the delegates should be permitted to keep individual gift items themselves. A gift to the unit as a whole was always a safe way to proceed, since all workers ostensibly benefited equally from such gestures. The truth, of course, was that nobody benefited at all.

Not surprisingly, this is no longer the way things work. The practice of giving individual mementos to members of a host group is now commonplace, among the Chinese themselves as well as among foreigners. It has always been the case in Taiwan, Hong Kong, and other places where Chinese people live and work. And it is perfectly acceptable on the mainland today, provided it is done in moderation.

In the late 1970s, when the PRC first opened its doors to the West, it was official policy to decline individual gifts from foreigners, and a worker who was found to have accepted any sort of present could get into a great deal of trouble. The reason was fear of corruption: Rich foreigners, so the argument went, could afford to offer substantial bribes and entice otherwise model Chinese workers into revealing state secrets or granting concessions in business.

Chinese policy has more recently been guided by a somewhat more moderate approach. There are rules governing what government and Party officials are permitted to accept, which some honor and others studiously ignore. Recognizing that policing a very restrictive policy is essentially impossible, the Chinese leadership no longer worries much about small gifts of nominal value—those of about $25 or less—and these may be retained by the recipients.

That's not always the way things happen, of course. One by-product of the open door policy instituted by the late Deng Xiaoping in 1979, as even the Chinese themselves will admit, has been an exponential rise in the incidence of official corruption. One constantly hears stories of larger gifts presented to Chinese decision-makers by business representatives eager to make a sale or close a deal, similar to practices employed elsewhere in the world. There are also Chinese officials who actively solicit such gifts.

There is unquestionably an increased willingness on the part of many Chinese to play fast and loose with the rules, and indeed, more and more instances of corruption are being exposed. Every once in a while the Chinese government will publicize the bringing to justice of a corrupt official in the hope that the case will serve as a negative example to would-be offenders. Cynics observe that if the government ever got really serious about corruption in its ranks there would be few officials left to serve.

The prevalence of corruption is understandable when you consider the paltry salaries earned by civil servants in China as compared to those earned by foreigners, overseas Chinese, local Chinese entrepreneurs, and even the leaders of profitable state-owned corporations. But to tar the entire mainland civil service with this brush is to do an injustice to those government officials who remain honest and committed to doing their jobs in an impartial way. It is probably true that corruption is a bigger problem on the provincial and local government levels than it is in the capital, though this is not to imply that no one in the central government is above reproach.

The government's bids to crack down on official corruption to date have smacked more of lip service than that of serious efforts at enforcement. It is true that high officials have occasionally been prosecuted and publicly removed from office, but these actions have sometimes had more to do with political infighting than they have with any serious efforts at routing out corruption. One-party rule, alas, is no crucible for reform in this disagreeable area.

Because gift-giving is an area in which common practice departs from the rules, it's hard to be categorical in giving advice on how best to proceed. It really depends on how comfortable you are wading through murky waters. The most conservative approach remains the traditional one: a single large gift for the whole group, presented to the leader either during a meeting or a banquet. Next would be individual gifts to all participants, presented together with a major organizational gift. The personal tokens may be put at the place settings before a banquet begins, and the overall gift presented ceremoniously at the appropriate moment. This approach is not really risky if the gifts are of nominal value.

On the more reckless end of the spectrum would be a very valuable gift presented in private to a powerful individual; the chances of this being construed as bribery if discovered are great. My personal practice is never to get involved in such corrupt activities. Bribery is mostly not necessary to do business in China, and when it is, one must wonder whether the recipients can be counted on to be honorable partners down the pike.

TIPPING

In Hong Kong, Macao, and Taiwan, you may, and to a certain extent are expected to, offer a cash gratuity to waiters, bellhops, and doormen. Except in deluxe hotels and restaurants, where service charges are often added into your bill anyway, tipping in these places generally means leaving behind some loose change and small bills; there is not really a set percentage as there is in many other parts of the world.

On the mainland, tipping has never been officially sanctioned. The government has traditionally seen it as an unpalatable vestige of the more exploitative aspects of capitalism, holding that the motivation for providing good service to visitors should be a commitment to doing one's job rather than cold cash. In the early days when foreigners were first permitted to visit the PRC, it was not unusual for a service person at a restaurant to chase a foreign guest for half a block simply to return a stray coin left on a table after a meal; it often did not even cross the person's mind that the money was meant for him or her.

It doesn't take much of an imagination to figure out that under such a system, service in China became notoriously indifferent, and occasionally downright surly. This is still the case in many state-owned establishments.

Two things changed, however. The first was the growth in private enterprises, specifically private restaurants. The proprietors of these establishments quickly realized that polite service was an advantage in a competitive world, and their employees—sometimes their family members—got the word. Even without tipping, you are far more likely to be treated courteously and solicitously in a private restaurant than in a state-owned establishment.

The second thing that changed was the preponderance not only of foreigners themselves, but of foreign-operated or foreign-managed establishments. These began to follow common international practice rather than local practice, and that generally consisted of adding a service charge on top of the charge for food and drink. Today a service charge is assessed at the better restaurants in major Chinese cities, though in truth, it doesn't generally find its way to the serving staff.

Tipping is still not customary in local restaurants, state-owned or otherwise, nor in taxis. Local Chinese do not do tip in these situations, nor do waiters, waitresses, or cabbies expect gratuities, though nobody will decline one, either. It is, however, becoming increasingly commonplace for foreigners to offer tips to the porters who carry their bags to their hotel room, or to service people who go out of their way to help them.

Whatever official policy dictates, there are often situations in which you wish to reward someone for a kindness, or for service above and beyond the call of duty. In such situations, it is best to take some precautions, because service personnel in some places are still at risk of being chastised for accepting gifts from foreign guests.

To reward someone who has been especially solicitous, first make sure you do it in private; no one else, especially colleagues of the person in question, should be present. Give cash, or else a gift that fits easily into a pocket, out of sight; some suggestions are given below. Don't pay attention to the one or two obligatory refusal gestures; place the gift in the person's pocket if necessary. On the other hand, if you sense a genuine and persistent reluctance to accept the gift, don't force the issue. Count on the Chinese to know better than you whether he or she is at any risk for receiving it.

What to Give

Chinese delegations visiting foreign countries often arrive with valises packed full of gifts. Companies, universities, or other organizations that host the group or simply meet with them are rewarded with these gift items. And generally speaking, the more the organization has done for the group, the more valuable will be the gift.

The Chinese are fond of giving objects of art and handicrafts produced in China. These may range from the sublime to the hideous; for every painstakingly crafted cloissonné vase, lacquerware serving piece, or hand-painted scroll there is a garish porcelain Buddha, an iridescent velvet wall hanging, or a clock that plays the theme from *Dr. Zhivago*. It is, however, the thought that counts, and no one can accuse the Chinese of not being thoughtful when it comes to gifts.

If you are giving a major gift to a Chinese organization, art objects are thus clearly acceptable. One approach is to try to give something created in your own country, and ideally something representative of local arts and crafts. Steuben glass, Revere silver, Wedgwood, or Hummel figurines, for example, would all be acceptable. Keep in mind, however, that many Chinese lack the criteria to evaluate objects of Western art, and probably wouldn't fully appreciate the quality of Steuben glass. A book featuring beautiful photographs of your native land would also be a good gift; Chinese who do not travel abroad can thumb through the pages and learn something of the world outside.

Another approach is to give something useful. If you are visiting the local harbor officials in a given city, for example, providing a book on port planning or one covering the latest techniques in the movement of container cargo would be a very practical present. In such a situation, don't worry if the book is written in English; if its contents are valuable to the unit, someone will be charged with translating relevant portions of it into Chinese. Appliances and battery-powered consumer electronics also qualify as useful gifts.

Still another appropriate memento is one that says something about your company. It might be a book about the history of your firm, or perhaps a model or sample of one of your products. If you are in China on a return visit, an album of photographs of your counterparts taken during their trip to your country is a sure winner. If you give a book, having your company's chairman or president inscribe it is an excellent idea; it's a signal to the Chinese that your visit to China has received attention at the highest levels of your organization.

Individual gifts should be small and, as mentioned previously, of modest value. Many items that companies regularly produce in quantity as giveaways are well received in China: pen and pencil sets, solar calculators, cigarette lighters, tape measures, pen-sized flashlights, penknives, inexpensive digital watches, leather folders, shirts, caps, and tote bags are all examples. By all means leave the company logo on; a logo changes a gift into a memento. If you give individual mementos, it's important to make sure that everyone receives something, so bring extras along just in case. Another excellent idea: tickets to local concerts or musical shows.

Gifts given to friends or those presented in nonbusiness situations can be more personal. Audiocassettes are always welcome; choose music representative of the type popular at home. Big crowd-pleasers include instant photos of guests, electronic datebook planners that use Chinese characters,

Western-produced books about Chinese art, and VCD recordings of English karaoke tunes. Foreign liquor and cigarettes are also highly appreciated; increasingly sophisticated Chinese businesspeople who have spent time in airport duty-free shops are well aware of the brands and prices of cognacs, brandies, and whiskies as well as foreign-made cigarettes.

For women, small makeup kits and skin creams of all descriptions are great gifts. I've also had success giving perfume, cologne, and other personal care products that, while increasingly easy to obtain in China, may still be quite expensive there.

What Not to Give

There are relatively few taboos about what constitutes an appropriate gift. One traditional prohibition revolves around clocks. The Chinese expression "to give a clock," which is rendered as *song zhong*, is a homonym for a phrase that means "to attend a dying parent." Though most Chinese don't really care, the very superstitious still balk at clocks as presents for this reason. Since it's easy enough to come up with other ideas, it is probably best to stay away from clocks. Similarly, cut flowers should be avoided as these are reminiscent of Chinese funerals, and green hats are to be eschewed, as a man who "wears a green hat" in China is being cuckolded by his wife.

You should also avoid giving gifts of excessive value. Because of the reciprocal obligation that surrounds gift-giving (see below), to give an extremely expensive present is often to put someone in the position of being unable to repay it in kind. Rendering someone unable to discharge an obligation can result in a loss of face.

Presents are generally wrapped in bright red, which is a festive color for the Chinese; they may be covered in other colors as well, but never in white. To the Chinese, white connotes death and mourning. This does not mean the color white may never appear in a magazine or a newspaper or on a garment; as a background color it is perfectly acceptable. But when it is the featured color, as in a white carnation or in all-white wrapping paper, it is to be avoided. If you lack wrapping paper, putting a red ribbon on a gift box is often all that is necessary.

PRESENTING GIFTS

There is a certain amount of ritual that goes along with presenting gifts. Most important, a custom common to many countries in the Far East dictates that any gift, even one a person plans to accept, should be refused at least once, and often as many as three times. A Chinese may even push a gift back at the giver, protesting loudly that he or she has been embarrassed by the gesture and can't possibly accept the item. This doesn't happen in formal situations, but can easily happen between friends.

Since this type of behavior is not common in the West, it's important to take it for what it really is. Don't withdraw the gift at this point. Continue to press it on the recipient through as many as three refusals. Only if you begin to sense that the protests are in earnest and that the individual genuinely does not want the item (for example, because he or she might get into trouble for receiving it, or may not want to be obligated to you) should you back off. While being rejected in this way is not a pleasant experience, it is not necessarily an embarrassing one. It's best afterward to continue to relate to the individual as if the incident never took place.

Like any other object, a gift should be given with both hands as a sign of courtesy. Individual gifts presented at banquets may be left at place settings, but organizational gifts must be presented formally, so remember the two-handed method.

If you are giving an organizational gift, the best time to present it is during your toast at a banquet—either one at which you are a guest, or, preferably, one hosted by you. You may also do this at the end of the meal, just prior to departure. A formal gift given in such a situation will never be refused. There should be no surprises here, however; it's always best to let someone on the Chinese side know that a gift is coming. This avoids the embarrassment of receiving a present empty-handed; it allows the other side to prepare a reciprocal gift.

It is not a Chinese custom to open gifts in the presence of the giver. However, the Chinese are flexible on this point. If your organization is presenting a major gift to a Chinese host group at a banquet and you wish them to open it in your presence, you might well explain to them that it is a Western custom to open the gift in front of the giver and that you would be pleased if the Chinese host would open the gift at that point. Your Chinese host will probably happily comply with your request.

There is something to be said for opening personal gifts at home, however. It does avoid ludicrous scenes of people oohing and aahing over gifts they never really wanted and do not really need. The Chinese are more pragmatic, and are less concerned with selecting individual gifts with the recipient's interests and idiosyncrasies in mind. It is not of vital importance that a gift be just what you wanted, or obviously selected with you and only you in mind. For a Chinese it truly is not the gift that counts, but the thought. As the Chinese say, *Li qing; renyi zhong*. It means "The gift is trifling, but the feeling is profound." Opening the gift in public would focus too much attention on the object itself, and not enough on the thought.

THE PRICE OF RECEIVING

The Chinese attach a price to the receipt of gifts, and this is as true of overseas Chinese as it is of their mainland brethren. Chinese often offer gifts when they are about to ask favors. This can be extremely unsubtle: An acquaintance with whom you have been out of touch for years may suddenly show up bearing a gift—a sure sign that you are about to be asked for a favor of some sort. A Chinese college professor I barely knew once showed up at my door with a neatly wrapped present. Once invited in and offered some tea, he eventually got to the point of the visit: Would I be willing to escort his daughter to the U.S. Embassy and negotiate for a visa for her?

Sometimes it is the favor that comes first, not the gift. If someone gets your brother a job, or helps your son get admission into a foreign university, or even helps you get a hard-to-get ticket for a train trip or a cultural performance, a token is often expected. The value of the gift should correlate roughly with the magnitude of the favor, except in hardship situations where the recipient can't afford much.

The line between gifts and bribes is in fact often a fine one in China. And although declining a gift can be awkward, if you feel a quid pro quo dynamic is being established as a result of your accepting a gift from someone, the best strategy is to decline the gift. If you have never done a favor for the person and don't intend to, life remains much less complicated if you stay away from the economy of obligations created by giving and receiving gifts.

Recap: Ten Caveats on Giving Gifts

1. Gifts are given to show esteem or gratitude, as souvenirs, as gratuities, or as payoffs in China. They discharge obligations, mark occasions, or accompany requests for favors.
2. Visiting groups are expected to give presents to their hosts. The conservative tack is to present one large gift to the host organization as a whole rather than a number of small gifts to its individual staff members.
3. Giving individual mementos to members of a host group is very common, however. The Chinese leadership permits individuals to keep small gifts of nominal value.
4. More and more Chinese are willing play fast and loose with the rules, but to give a very valuable gift to a powerful individual is still a risky proposition.
5. Tipping has never been officially sanctioned on the mainland, and is not the custom in state-owned enterprises or in private establishments. However, service charges are generally added to bills in better restaurants, and tips to hotel porters and other service personnel are appreciated and will generally not be refused. Standard practice is at odds with the rules here, so you should use your own discretion.

6. One way to reward someone for service or a favor is to give a small gift. Wait for a private moment, and give something that fits easily into a pocket.
7. Chinese may make as many as three refusal gestures when they are offered gifts; only if you sense genuine reluctance should you stop offering one.
8. Objects of art are acceptable business gifts for Chinese organizations, though many Chinese lack the criteria to evaluate their true worth, artistic or otherwise. Useful gifts and company mementos are also acceptable. Individual gifts should be small and of modest value, such as pens, calculators, lighters, tape measures, and tote bags. Gifts to friends may be more personal.
9. Don't give clocks, cut flowers, or green hats (for superstitious reasons), and avoid gifts of excessive value. Wrap presents in bright red if possible, never in white. Give gifts with both hands as a sign of courtesy. Don't expect your gift to be opened in your presence unless you specifically request it.
10. Gifts often carry unspoken obligations, such as the granting of favors. If you have never done a favor for a person and don't intend to, decline his or her gift politely. Gifts given in return for favors should correlate roughly with the magnitude of the favor.

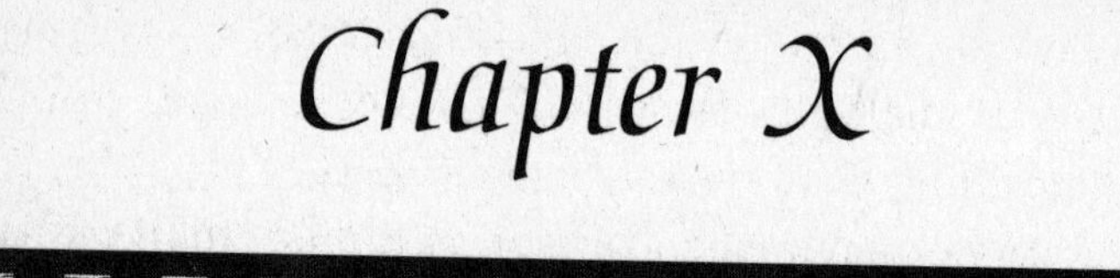

Chapter X

Guanxi: *Grease for the Wheels of China*

FORGET THE ORGANIZATION CHARTS. FORGET THE FORMAL structures that make up any Chinese corporation or government unit, or any explicit set of regulations or procedures that specify who is supposed to do what to whom. As anyone with a modicum of experience in the PRC can tell you, the key to getting anything important accomplished in China lies not in the formal order, but rather in who you know, and in how that person views his or her obligations to you.

The Chinese call this concept *guanxi*. It's a term that literally means "relationships," but that in this context translates far better as "connections." Of course it is by no means unique to China: Western society is hardly without its own concept of "pull." It's just that the Chinese have raised *guanxi* to a high art. It pervades the social order, and nowhere more than in today's PRC.

If you have *guanxi*, there is little you can't get accomplished, even if it is technically—or sometimes even brazenly—against the rules. If you *don't* have *guanxi*, on the other hand, the opposite may be true. Your life is likely to be a series of long lines and tightly closed doors, and a maze of administrative and bureaucratic hassles.

Under orthodox communism, the *guanxi* system was very much a reality, but the stakes were generally fairly low, at least by today's standards. It was an era in which most Chinese were not permitted to go abroad, when it was nearly impossible to change one's work unit, and when there were few goods in the stores worth having and even less money to buy them. Back then, common people tended to use *guanxi* to get access to theater tickets, the use of a work unit automobile for a personal errand, or commodities or petty favors that, while not easy to come by, did not involve large outlays of cash.

Today, however, in an era of multimillion-dollar deals, fierce competition, and international travel, *guanxi* can count for a great deal more. Companies, foreign and local alike, spend heavily to establish and maintain relationships with those who run and influence China's powerful government organizations and state-owned conglomerates. The payoff may be personal, ranging from a job or foreign university admission for a senior official's child to a discreet but illegal transfer of funds into a Hong Kong bank account. Or it may be organizational, such as cutting a Chinese unit in on a deal as a means to secure the connection. The outsiders then count on the *guanxi* they have established to protect them from overburdensome regulations or costly changes in government policy, or to prolong the terms of a profitable sweetheart deal.

A Very Personal Thing

While *guanxi* may be organizational, at its heart it is a relationship between two people who are expected, more or less, to give as good as they get. A Chinese with a problem, personal or organizational, naturally turns to his or her *guanxiwang* (relationship network) for help. Surely among this array of acquaintances—relatives, classmates, colleagues, neighbors, and friends—is someone who has pull at this hospital, that school, or that regulatory body.

If you were angling for a job in the film industry, for example, the first question would be "Whom do I know who can get me in the door at the Shanghai Film Studio?" If no one came to mind, the next question would be "Whom does one of my friends know?" Part of a Chinese's responsibility to those with whom he or she has *guanxi* is to offer access to others in his or her network. In other words, if you approach me for help, the "deliverable" may not be a favor; it may, rather, be a request to someone *else* I know to do you the favor, based on my say-so.

This is why Chinese work so assiduously to cultivate new friends, especially friends in high or strategic places who may be useful sometime in the future. The expression *Duo yige guanxi, duo yitiao lu*—"One more connection offers one more road to take"—really says it all. Foreigners, who are presumed by many to be wealthy and well connected, are particularly susceptible to being recruited in this way.

This is not to cast aspersions on the motives of any given Chinese about to enter into a new friendship. Like people everywhere, Chinese make friends with people they find interesting or attractive, and no ulterior motive need necessarily be present. But it is also surely true that a person's position, power, money, social status, and connections all factor into a Chinese person's assessment of his or her attractiveness as a friend, as they would anywhere else in the world, only perhaps more so.

Given the importance of *guanxi* in getting access to the best things in life, if a Chinese enters a new situation and finds him or herself without any *guanxi*, the first order of business is generally to establish some. This is precisely why Chinese who move overseas—to places as far away as North America or Europe or as close to home as Southeast Asia or Hong Kong—have traditionally established affiliative organizations based on place of origin in China (for example, the Ningbo Residents Association) or even on surname (for example, the Mei Family Association).

Never mind that by no stretch of the imagination can all people who bear the same Chinese surname possibly be assumed to be blood relatives. The common surname—or the common county or province of origin—is in fact little more than an excuse to help new arrivals establish some beneficial relationships, get established, find a place to live and a job, or borrow some money.

The need to establish *guanxi* as a first order of business happens in China even at the most prosaic level. A Chinese friend who moved to Beijing from a remote province and who was determined to find work in Beijing faced a major hurdle because he had no *guanxiwang* in the capital. Even today, it's difficult to find decent employment in China without one, since jobs too frequently go not to those best qualified, but those best connected. My friend's solution was to strike up a friendship with his landlady, who eventually helped him find a sales job at a nearby clothing store that was managed by a friend of hers. As a Chinese, he knew instinctively that the way to find a job was *not* to pound the pavement or to make cold calls; these would probably have been fruitless wastes of time, unlikely to have forced open any doors. Rather, it was to spend time and energy building relationships in order to find his way to someone who would open a door *for* him.

What *Guanxi* Can Do

There are few rules in China that can't be broken, or at least bent, by people with the right *guanxi*. For several months before and after the handover of Hong Kong to Chinese sovereignty, for example, the PRC government imposed restrictions on visits to Hong Kong by citizens of the mainland in the ostensible interest of security. The enforcement mechanism was at the airports and borders; PRC citizens bound for Hong Kong were turned away by immigration officials unless they possessed a special permit. A Chinese friend of mine found this out the hard way: She was turned back at Beijing's Capital Airport and not permitted to board a plane for Hong Kong, even though she had a perfectly legitimate business reason for going.

Undeterred, she set out the next day to renew an acquaintance her father had with a senior official at the airport. She took him to lunch, and in the course of the meal told him of her problem. She didn't even need to ask for his help directly. He understood the situation completely and personally escorted her through the immigration line. End of problem.

Or consider the story of a friend of mine who needed to

clear a shipment of goods through customs in Shanghai, which shows clearly the power of *guanxi* to grease gears that have ground to a complete halt. While my friend's company was duly registered to do business in Guangzhou, his Shanghai office was technically a representative office, which was enjoined from profit-making activities. Because of this, Shanghai customs did not believe it was empowered to clear the shipment—or else it simply chose not to do so.

It soon became clear that no amount of arguing with the customs official in charge was going to change his contention that the paperwork should be done in Guangzhou, and so the goods just sat there. The solution came in the form of a friend of my friend who was in the freight forwarding business and whose *guanxi* with the Shanghai Customs Bureau was excellent. All it took was a quick phone call; the shipment cleared the next day.

A Chinese friend has pointed out to me that one important reason for the pervasiveness of the *guanxi* system in China is the relative lack of a reliable legal system. In a nation that has traditionally had relatively little use for laws, personal power has always been the key to getting things accomplished. Conversely, the entrenched nature of the *guanxi* system has proven to be one of the most powerful obstacles to establishing anything resembling rule of law in the PRC, and is probably the biggest headache of would-be legal reformers in China. Even when they live in countries where the legal system is well developed and the law impartially enforced, Chinese still rely heavily on their *guanxi* networks.

Guanxi also offers protection. China is full of people—and places—said to have been "protected" by the late premier Zhou Enlai or others during the turmoil of the Cultural

Revolution. Zhou, while attacked, never completely lost his prestige even during the height of the madness, and his long, protective shadow saved many from persecution and destruction.

Conversely, people *not* deserving of refuge sometimes get it through *guanxi* as well. Associates of deposed Beijing mayor Chen Xitong reportedly got away with rampant acts of corruption because while Chen was in power, no one dared blow the whistle on them and risk retaliation. It was only after Chen was arrested that anyone dared clean house in the municipal government, and many were brought to justice.

Good *guanxi* is a renewable resource. A Chinese friend of mine who had lived abroad for a decade and returned to Beijing lost no time in finding out exactly where her university classmates were working. She had been out of touch with most of them for several years, and many of them turned out to have risen to high or strategically important positions. Despite the hiatus, the *guanxi* was very much still there for the renewing, as classmate relationships are very important in China. She lost little time in calling on these former friends for favors and information.

But *guanxi* can also be an exhaustible resource. An initial favor is surely granted when it is owed, and is also often provided based on no more than the promise that the ledger will someday be put into balance. But one cannot continue to seek favors indefinitely based on a historical debt, because at such time as the debt is judged to be paid, the sense of obligation may cease.

If Mr. Wang is instrumental in helping Ms. Liu find housing in Beijing's notoriously tight real estate market, she will surely be good for the occasional introduction or discount in the future. But at some point, perhaps after Mr. Wang asks for a very large favor, Ms. Liu may well decide that he has been paid back adequately for services rendered, and feel no more obligation to him. Whenever possible, therefore, Chinese instinctively try to keep the economy of favors in rough balance over time.

It is such a reflexive reaction for a Chinese to fall back on his or her *guanxiwang* that he or she may call on favors when they may not even be necessary. I once asked an employee in my company to get me a very basic piece of information—the name of China's third largest city. I figured it would be a relatively easy task to look it up in a reference book or make a quick phone call, and expected him to report back to me within a few moments. When more than an hour passed and there was no word from him, I tracked him down and asked him what he had managed to find out. The answer was nothing.

Why? Because his friend at the State Statistical Bureau was out of the office that morning and wouldn't be back until the afternoon. He had given no thought to asking whoever answered the phone at the Bureau for the piece of information in question. Quite possibly he had a clearer notion than I did that that would have been a fruitless endeavor. Even for such a simple problem as identifying China's third largest city, *guanxi* was the path of choice.

Foreigners and *Guanxi*

Guanxi is not only a catalyst for getting things accomplished in China, it is equally often also a formidable obstacle.

When a foreign company sued a Chinese firm that had taken delivery of a piece of merchandise but failed to pay for it, the local court found in favor of the plaintiff. But when the customer was found to be without sufficient funds to pay for the goods and the foreign company decided to go after the offender's parent company, it all fell apart.

Why? Because suing the parent company meant approaching the court in the district in which the parent was domiciled. And that court had absolutely no interest in taking the case. As a low-level court official explained, "We don't even know you, and owe you nothing. But we've got an excellent relationship with the company you want to sue. Why should we risk it for you?"

Why, indeed? What this case shows—in addition to the power of *guanxi*, and to the lack of an independent judiciary in China—is also the importance to foreigners and foreign organizations of building up *guanxi* networks of their own in China. It is only the naïve and uninitiated who leave all the *guanxi*-building to their Chinese partners. Good relationships with the customs bureau, the tax bureau, the local bureau of industry and commerce and the myriad of other regulatory organizations charged with oversight of foreigners and their affairs are as good as gold in China.

The good news is that in today's China such relationships are well within the grasp of foreigners who wish to cultivate them. Often all it takes is an overture—a conversation, a meal, or a favor. No longer is one's ability to get things done dependent on which organization is one's official host in China. In the old days, all foreigners were considered guests, permitted to reside in China only through the good offices of one Chinese government organization or another. If you had the misfortune of being the guest of a unit without much clout, woe betide you if you needed access to a scarce commodity like a room in a leading hotel or an airplane or train ticket to a popular destination. Those went only to guests of units—or individuals within units—with *guanxi*.

Foreigners who live and work in China may become integrated into the *guanxiwang* of those with whom they come in contact—sometimes unwittingly. As components of this network, they are expected to play by Chinese rules, which are not always to their liking. In particular, there may be a host of expectations on the part of those who befriend them that may not necessarily be clear at the outset of the relationship, and that may be unacceptable to the foreigner.

The Chinese tend to extrapolate from their own system and assume that the rest of the world works along a similar set of principles, and this often means that they view foreign friends as windows to benefits in the world outside China. Thus, if you are Canadian, you are assumed to be able to coax favors out of the Canadian Embassy or local consulate, and acquire admissions into Canadian universities as well as visas for Chinese who wish to visit, study in, or emigrate to, Canada. You may well be asked to deliver on such an expectation, however unfeasible it is that you will be able to do so. And if you don't deliver, you may be labeled as *bugou pengyou*, "not enough of a friend."

Then, too, the Chinese often do not distinguish clearly between the world of the personal and the world of the organizational. This means a personal friend may well ask for an organizational favor. Since you and I know each other well, for example, would you please send your company's travel business to my friend's travel agency? Or, since my mother and your mother were classmates, will you use your influence to get a high-ranking official to come to the event my organization is planning? The distinction between the personal and the professional is obvious to foreigners and often matters a great deal to them; it is, however, one that is often lost on the Chinese.

It is important to note that Chinese expectations notwithstanding, foreigners are well within their rights to draw their own lines as to what they are and are not prepared to deliver for those with whom they have established *guanxi*. Even though the Chinese may be willing to bend the rules, this does not mean that foreigners must do the same. In my experience, Chinese can be made to understand my own ethical limits if I take the trouble to explain them. I generally try to steer clear of those who cannot, as more often than not I find such relationships problematical.

Chinese may also differ from Westerners in the level of delicacy with which they approach asking for favors. The establishment and use of *guanxi* may be accomplished very deftly, but equally often it can be entirely lacking in subtlety. When someone you know but have not seen for months or even years shows up on your doorstep bearing a gift, as illustrated in the previous chapter, it isn't hard to figure out that the inevitable request for a favor is coming. With Westerners the gift is much more likely to come later, and it would be viewed as déclassé even to allude to a gift before the favor is granted. Westerners are far more coy in acknowledging that any tit-for-tat is going on in a relationship; the Chinese, on the other hand, see these things in far more pragmatic terms.

Chinese generally feel freer to ask for favors earlier in a relationship than Westerners do. To be sure, only an uncouth

Chinese will hit a stranger up for a favor on the first meeting, but by the second or third get-together a new friend is generally considered fair game for a request. One does not want to give the impression of giving the bum's rush, even if that is exactly what is going on, so one waits a decent interval before putting new *guanxi* to work. But in the eyes of many foreigners, the Chinese often accelerate the definition of "decent."

Unlike foreigners, who may feel quite put upon when asked for favors—especially personal favors that involve the use of organizational resources—Chinese are often very eager to be of service if they have it in their power to assist. This is true for two reasons. First, because doing a favor for a friend is inherently face-enhancing; it shows you are a person of some means or ability. And second, because every favor you do builds your credit column on the balance sheet that governs your relationship with the requester. You are, in essence, banking chits against the day that you will be the one who needs the favor.

GUANXI FOR SALE

The importance of *guanxi* in navigating the bureaucracy in China cannot be overstated, and in recent years it has become a commodity that is increasingly for sale. Many of the sons and daughters of high-ranking cadres, in particular, have set up "consulting" shops or "service" companies and offered their ability to mobilize their own *guanxiwang*, and those of their parents, to the highest bidder. Even the children of former officials not currently in favor can make a living by becoming intermediaries in business deals, since their own *guanxi* networks were generally established as early as elementary school, and include a full complement of the offspring of still-powerful senior cadres.

Nor are foreigners excluded from this game. Several former foreign government officials who established relationships with counterpart Chinese officials while they were in office now operate high-priced consultancies through which they essentially sell this access to companies in need of it. One of the reasons this works so well is the loyalty on the part of Chinese officials to their old friends. While the foreign government official may now be out of power, he or she is still likely to be granted an audience with a Chinese official if it is requested—even if the purpose of the meeting is clearly to advance the fortunes of a corporate client.

Much has been made of the Chinese preference for doing business with old friends, and while this bromide can surely be overstated—one may qualify as an "old friend" as early as the second meeting—the statement is essentially true. While Westerners typically have a decided aversion to the thought of selling something to a friend or relative, the Chinese actually have a preference for it. For every Westerner who would rather peddle his car to a used car lot for less money than sell it to a cousin, there's a Chinese who feels that there are always issues and conflicts in business, and that the very connectedness he or she feels to a friend or relative can help resolve these conflicts.

Similarly, a Chinese is generally far happier to hire a relative than a stranger, because he or she believes it diminishes the danger of malfeasance. A blood relative, after all, can be counted on to think twice about doing anything that would cause his or her patron to lose face or to lose assets. A Westerner would probably worry about being accused of nepotism for doing the very same thing. He or she might be almost apologetic about recommending a relative or a close personal friend for a job, bending over backward to point out the person's qualifications for the job, driving home the point that the candidate is not being endorsed merely because of the relationship.

Consider the case of a very lucrative contract that was under discussion for more than a year between a large Chinese state-owned enterprise and two multinational firms. After months of formal negotiations, the Chinese unit selected one of the competitors to continue the discussions. It happened to be the one that was then employing the son of the principal negotiator on the Chinese side—and at a very substantial salary. This despite the fact that the chosen supplier's equipment was demonstrably less well adapted to work with Chinese equipment already in place. And also despite the fact that the son's position with the winning company was well known to everyone on the Chinese side. Either no one felt that the deal was compromised by what would appear to a Westerner as an obvious conflict of interest, or—far more likely—no one dared pipe up because of the prestige of the chief Chinese negotiator.

Guanxi in high places is something to which everyone aspires, because those at the top have power and fairly large and powerful *guanxiwang* of their own. But *guanxi* need not necessarily be high-level to be effective. When a major multinational corporation failed to file paperwork in time to ensure annual renewal of its registration for its representative office, the company was offered a stark choice by the State Administration for Industry and Commerce (SAIC): Pay a confiscatory fine or lose the registration, and with it the company's ability to operate legally in China.

After much hand-wringing, the management decided to try back-channel routes to the SAIC through *guanxi*, but none of the senior advisors retained by the company were able to help; though they knew ministers and State Council members, they didn't know any local SAIC officials. Ever more desperate as the days ticked away, the management eventually discussed the problem openly with all of the company's employees, at which time an entry-level clerk came forward. It turned out that she had gone to high school with the daughter of a local SAIC director. After several phone calls and a banquet, the registration was renewed, with no fines paid.

Such is the power of *guanxi*.

Recap: Eight Tips on *Guanxi*

1. The concept of *guanxi* (connections) is not unique to China, but it is vital to getting important things accomplished there. Local and foreign companies spend heavily to establish and maintain relationships with influential people. The payoff may be personal or organizational.
2. At its heart, *guanxi* is a tit-for-tat relationship between two people. Chinese naturally turn to their relationship networks for help, so they work hard to cultivate friends in high or strategic places. If a Chinese finds him- or her-

self without *guanxi*, the first order of business is to establish some.

3. One reason for the pervasiveness of the *guanxi* system on the mainland is the relative lack of a reliable legal system. But it is also important in areas outside China, where the legal system is more developed.
4. Good *guanxi* is a renewable resource and can be reestablished even after much time has passed. But it may also be an exhaustible resource if the ledger between two people does not remain in approximate balance.
5. *Guanxi* is well within the grasp of foreigners who wish to cultivate it. Often all it takes is an overture—a conversation, a meal, or a favor. Foreigners who live and work in China may become integrated into relationship networks, where they are expected to play by Chinese rules. Nonetheless, they are within their rights to draw their own lines as to what they are and are not prepared to deliver.
6. The Chinese assume the rest of the world works along a similar set of principles, and they sometimes view foreign friends as windows to benefits in the world outside China. They also often do not distinguish clearly between the world of the personal and the world of the organizational, which means that a personal friend may well ask for an organizational favor.
7. Chinese generally feel freer to ask for favors earlier in a relationship than Westerners do. Unlike foreigners, who may feel quite put upon when asked for favors—especially personal favors that involve the use of organizational resources—Chinese are often very eager to be of

service if they have it in their power to assist. In recent years *guanxi* has even become a commodity for sale.

8. Chinese prefer to do business with, and even to hire, those with whom they have *guanxi*, as contrasted to an aversion to doing this among Westerners. They believe it diminishes the danger of problems, and makes solving them much easier when they do arise.

Mianzi: About Face

WHY WILL A CHINESE OF MINIMAL MEANS ENTER INTO MORtal combat with a well-heeled friend over a check in an expensive restaurant, but watch in abject horror as a group of Americans at the next table uses a calculator to determine who owes what—down to the penny? Why will a Chinese employee who wants to quit an unpleasant job deal only in pleasantries when she faces the boss, even as her Western counterpart uses the exit interview to detail all the offenses of which the boss has been guilty?

And why will a Chinese manager stick stubbornly to an announced policy, even when subsequent events prove it to have been irretrievably misguided, when a Western boss would long since have reversed himself?

The answer is face. These seeming anomalies are all about face.

I've often wondered if it could possibly be mere coincidence that the term "face" has so many meanings common to English and Chinese. In both tongues, it can mean not only the area between the forehead and the chin, and not only a flat surface like the top of a table, but also an intangible commodity that is vital to a person's reputation, dignity, and prestige. In this last area, however, the Chinese concept is better defined than the Western one. Westerners are accustomed to the twin concepts of "losing" and "saving" face; these are metaphors we use and understand. But the Chinese do us one better; they are also very adept at "giving" face—enhancing someone else's esteem through compliments, flattery, or a show of respect.

Face, or *mianzi*, is arguably one of the three key motivators that govern behavior in the PRC these days, the others being money and power. But the three are related; if one uses money and power, as many Chinese do, to live well—to wear nice clothes, dine at fine restaurants, buy nice things, and generally find ways to demonstrate one's wealth or one's clout to others—then one is using them principally for the sake of face.

No one can say how much money has been wasted, how many people toppled from power, or how many friendships have been destroyed over something that belongs so utterly to the realm of the abstract rather than the concrete. Yet to Chinese, and to most of their Asian brethren, *mianzi* is deadly serious business, and no less so for its lack of tangibility. Those who wish to live, work, or do business in China ignore it at their peril.

Certainly mainland Chinese have no monopoly on concern for face. All cultures probably have some version of this concept, and most Asians surely worry about it to a greater or lesser extent. But China, emerging from decades of ideological repression and eradication of traditional cultural values, seems to be reembracing some of her ancestral habits with an extraordinary fervor these days. Less Westernized than other Asian cultures, and more xenophobic than many, China in the late 1990s seems hell-bent on a return to traditional values. And *mianzi* ranks high on that list.

Face Losers

Fragile commodity that it is, face can easily be lost, and in a myriad of ways. It ought to be obvious that a public insult, chastisement, or similar affront to personal dignity generally results in a humiliating loss of face. But the trigger needn't be so extreme. If you simply contradict someone in front of another, face may be lost. Or if you decline someone's invitation to dinner on a weak pretext, it can be read as a loss of face for the host.

Even the simple act of saying no to someone who requests something can be interpreted as an assault on *mianzi*, which is why when a Chinese must rebuff an entreaty, it is usually done by labeling it "inconvenient" or "difficult" rather than rejecting it out of hand. The meaning is the same, but in the first case, face is preserved, while in the latter case the person doing the requesting can be seen to have lost some, because a request was directly refused.

Failing to accord someone respect he or she deserves—or *thinks* he or she deserves—is also the stuff of which a loss of *mianzi* is made. The board of directors of a Beijing-based joint venture recently elected a new general manager. The person chosen was, in fact, the very candidate recommended by the Chinese industrial bureau to which the factory reported. But when it came time to swear in the new officer, no one thought to invite the bureau director to the ceremony. Never mind that he was not an officer of the corporation and hence had no particular need or right to be there. Leaving him out made it appear that he did not matter, and that was seen as an unforgivable slight.

Losing face isn't always the result of what *others* do to *you*, however; you are perfectly capable of losing it all by yourself. Losing your temper in public is a face loss. In fact, losing control of yourself in any way—whether anger, grief, angst, or any other emotion gets the better of you—always constitutes serious damage to *mianzi*. This includes drinking alcohol to the point of losing self-control. That's one good reason that it's best to moderate your drinking at banquets.

Rescinding an order that has already been issued can also be construed as being hazardous to one's *mianzi*. This is one reason that it often seems to outsiders to take an interminable period of time before Chinese leaders decide anything. Since face hangs in the balance, all options must be weighed and all eventualities considered. *Mianzi* is also why Chinese leaders may cling adamantly to set policies, even when subsequent events prove them irrelevant or misguided. To change one's mind is to appear to succumb to pressure or to admit error, either of which amounts to a loss of face. Often the only way to justify an abrupt about-face, in fact, is to invent a face-saving fiction.

Truth and Face

Losing face at someone else's behest is justification for some form of retaliation if opportunity permits. The price exacted may be as low as an apology or as high as a corresponding loss of face on the other side. And neither truth nor accuracy count for much when a major loss of face is involved.

For example, getting fired constitutes a major loss of *mianzi* in China today, since it amounts to a public statement that one is not adequate to one's job. It is especially sensitive in a socialist country in which, until quite recently, firing had been virtually unknown for forty years.

When a Chinese woman I know discovered she was about to be terminated for cause, she quickly attempted to turn the dismissal into a resignation, ranting very publicly among her colleagues about problems with her boss and her unwillingness to continue to work for such a poorly managed company. Her intent was to set up a smoke screen to obscure the real issue, which was her own poor job performance. Even though no one who knew her was fooled, it nonetheless set the stage for her to walk out with her head high—and her face intact—regardless of the facts of the case.

Quitting, too, has implications for *mianzi*. A Western woman I know was furious when she discovered that a Taiwanese woman who quit working for her had gone to work for a competitor. She was angry because at her exit interview, the employee had cited her need to stay home with her child as the reason for her departure. To the Westerner it looked like dishonesty, plain and simple. But what was *really* going on, and what the foreign boss didn't understand, was that the Chinese woman was quitting because she found the work environment intolerable. Telling the boss that it was all about staying at home was the path that preserved the boss's face, even though it was based on a lie.

Truth is no match for *mianzi*, and unless it serves someone's purpose, it almost always loses out when the two go head-to-head.

Organizational Face

Face is by no means only an individual asset. Organizations have face, too. Ministries, corporations, and bureaus all have reputations to worry about; so do entire countries. Not long ago, an American company got a taste of national ire when it inadvertently published a map of its China operations that entirely omitted Taiwan. The firm was severely chastised by a Chinese ministry that believed that, against the backdrop of a U.S.-China relationship strained at the time by wrangling over the Taiwan issue, a loss of face for China had occurred. In the eyes of the Chinese ministry, nothing short of a public apology by the offending company would set the matter right.

Such patriotism runs deep among Chinese today for a host of reasons. The first is a fundamental xenophobia that is based in history and is never very far from the surface. To this basic distrust of foreigners, add pride in a rich history of accomplishments poised against a decided feeling of inferiority in the face of the indisputable technological superiority of the West today as well as a couple of hundred years of humiliation at the hands of Western powers. Finally, given the total lack of enthusiasm for any political ideology that characterizes PRC Chinese in the 1990s, what remains is jingoism. It is strong enough to color the Chinese view of nearly any situation involving foreigners, justified or not.

For example, at an event I attended recently, a foreigner who had had too much to drink got into an argument with a Chinese and punched him in the face. Had the altercation been between two Chinese, it would doubtless have been mediated by those on the spot, with blame assigned, justice dispensed, and the matter settled relatively quickly and easily.

But because it was a foreigner who did the punching, the situation escalated into a full-blown international incident. The "foreign devil" was denounced by onlookers as having insulted the Chinese people as a whole, and the matter ultimately required mediation by the public security bureau. A grave threat to national "face" was detected where only a silly disagreement between two people had existed. In this case, money had to change hands to set the matter right.

Face is also very much present in business transactions—even simple price negotiations. While state-owned corporations are seldom able to offer substantial discounts, it is a rare individual enterprise that does *not* offer them, especially to favorite customers, friends and relatives, and those who buy in bulk. Most merchants routinely quote prices considerably higher than what they expect to get so they can offer a discount to buyers who demand just a little bit of *mianzi* to make them feel good about a transaction or look good to others. And the sellers generally expect reciprocal treatment when the tables are turned.

For instance, a friend of mine was bargaining for an objet d'art at an antique market a few months ago, but there was still a gap of about 200 *renminbi* between the asking and selling prices. He felt that his top offer was all the object was worth, and declined to go higher. This transaction had, of course, by then attracted its share of gapers and kibitzers, and while my friend eventually prevailed and the object changed hands, the proprietor chastised him before he left. The crime? Failing to give the proprietor face by upping his final offer, even if only nominally. The hawker's face had been lost, presumably, in the eyes of the observers and his immediate neighbors at the bazaar.

Multiply that antique dealer's discomfort about a hundredfold and you have an approximation of the magnitude of face that can be at stake in transactions in which state-owned corporations have large sums of money at risk. When Chinese negotiators lose sleep, one of the things they worry about most is being accused of not pressing hard enough for the best deal. Because criticism from above translates into a tremendous loss of face, and since direct retaliation is generally impossible in such situations, the recipient is forced to live in shame.

Foreigners and Face

Even diplomatic relations are often explainable, at least in part, purely in terms of face. Witness the 1995 brouhaha over PRC president Jiang Zemin's trip to the United States. He wound up meeting Bill Clinton at a "working meeting" in New York, his Washington trip being canceled because the Chinese side demanded nothing less than full state visit treatment—twenty-one-gun salute, state dinner at the White House; the works. The U.S. administration didn't feel it could accept these terms at that time if it wished to avoid Congressional reproach, but Jiang's people didn't feel they could face their own critics at home with anything less. Face, with a clear political tint, was operating on both sides of this equation. The state visit didn't ultimately occur until late 1997, when bilateral relations had improved considerably.

So, too, does face play a critical role when, for example, the U.S. government publicly puts China on notice to respond to a demand—to improve its human rights record, step up enforcement of its intellectual property laws, or something similar. It is precisely the American need to play these disputes out in public that makes it so troublesome for the Chinese to comply with U.S. ultimatums, even when it is very much in China's interest to do so. Concessions that may be made relatively easily behind closed doors are almost impossible to extract when the Chinese government feels its face is at stake. In such situations, the government would prefer to shoot itself in the foot, to mix metaphors, rather than lose face.

Foreigners may think they are immune to machinations involving face, but in fact it is easy for them to get caught up in the game. A foreign company I know wanted to set up a meeting with a Chinese minister for one of its senior officers. The Chinese ministry turned down the meeting twice, however, offering vice ministers as a substitute for the minister, who was always either unavailable, too busy, or out of town.

After two tries, the company still wished to have the meeting, but declined to ask for it again for fear of another refusal. Instead, the firm's Beijing representative worked through intermediaries to find out if such a request would be entertained *if* it were to be lodged a third time. A positive answer to this question would result in an immediate formal request; a negative answer would obviate the need for a potentially face-losing third try.

When interacting with the Chinese, foreigners are often swayed by the Chinese obsession with face. But to most Westerners, face is neither as important nor as well-developed a concept as it is in China. Chinese people spend far more time thinking about face, and see its relevance in far more situations, than foreigners do. To them, face is pervasive, and always a matter of grave importance. The Chinese can be counted on to view their human interactions through the lens of face; each and every one represents an opportunity to give, receive, save, or lose *mianzi*. Thus a casual comment or an innocent joke may be assigned extraordinary weight.

Then too, Western culture's emphasis on the individual—as contrasted with the group-centeredness of Asian societies—relegates the notion of "face" to a lower priority. It is not hard to conceive of a "rugged individualist" in the West who cares relatively little about relationships with other people. Given enough food to eat, money to spend, and a certain level of emotional fulfillment, such a person could conceivably live quite happily, even if disliked by others in the community for one reason or another. America is full of such people.

Such a situation would be unthinkable for a Chinese, however. No one in China would call a life complete or balanced if it did not include a high degree of overt respect and acceptance from others. Getting and keeping face simply occupies a much higher priority for a Chinese.

Put another way, if face were not of such overwhelming importance, people as practical as the Chinese would not devote so much time, effort, or money to trying to acquire it.

Face Givers

Things that make others look up to you, or be envious of you, also confer face on you.

There is, first of all, face in titles, which is why forms of address have always been vitally important to the Chinese (see Chapter 3). Instructing your son to call a friend "uncle" (*bobo* or *shushu*) is to do honor to the friend, for "uncle" is a respectful term that acknowledges both his age and his closeness to your family. Calling Vice Bureau Director Wang, "Bureau

Director Wang," or even just "Bureau Director," is also face-enhancing. This kind of title inflation isn't exactly accurate, but accuracy is not what you are going for here. He'll surely be glad to hear it, for it enhances his *mianzi*. Because there is so much face involved, Chinese often push hard to get impressive titles to put on their business cards, regardless of their actual responsibilities in an organization. The presumption is that they will get more attention and deference if their position sounds exalted enough.

Humbling yourself is another way to give face. The Chinese who writes a letter to a university professor and signs it "Your student" is doing precisely this. He may never have met the professor, still less taken a course from the person. He may not even be much younger than the professor. But in setting himself up as the inferior—the "student"—he is conferring prestige on the teacher—that is, giving face.

Things that build the ego give face. When a "somebody"—a government official, a well-known individual, or someone of accomplishment—condescends to attend an event sponsored by a "nobody," face is given. Doing a favor for a stranger who is introduced to you by a close friend confers *mianzi* on the introducer, since a benefit—the favor—was received solely on the strength of the connection to this person. Praising someone to his or her boss is also face-enhancing for the person in question, and especially so if the object of the compliment is present when it is delivered.

One-upmanship is also all about face enhancement, and the Chinese play this game as enthusiastically as anybody. Ten years ago no one would have predicted that Chinese in the PRC with severely limited incomes would eschew basic, functional products in favor of those bearing designer labels. But this is exactly what has happened in the China of the 1990s.

The propensity of Chinese to wear newly acquired wealth on their backs is eloquent testimony to the power of face. Money that might be set aside for a rainy day or spent on something functional is instead used to purchase a pair of sunglasses or a designer suit that may be worn with the label on the lens—or on the sleeve—to demonstrate its foreign origin. Or cash is spent on the myriad pirated designer goods turned out by Chinese factories—jackets, purses, wallets, watches—in the hopes that others may be hoodwinked into thinking they are real.

By contrast, Chinese have a hard time understanding why Westerners, and more particularly Americans, can often be spotted on the street wearing worn-out clothing, jeans with holes in the knees, or simply inexpensive, casual clothes. What earthly reason could one have for dressing *below* one's station in life? In a nation where poor people have no choice but to wear rags, dressing well is serious business.

A nice place to live is also face-enhancing. If you don't have one, you must somehow work around it. A close Chinese friend of fifteen years has *never* invited me to his home. Once, at Chinese New Year, he muttered something about his home not being very attractive or comfortable. He then brought me some food his wife had cooked, which we ate together at my house. Far better, from his point of view, than showing me his, since he was clearly ashamed of it. Since many Chinese homes aren't much to look it, Chinese often entertain their friends at restaurants—and the more expensive, the better.

There's plenty of face in good food. Going to a famous restaurant and ordering shark's fin soup or some other costly entrée, or inviting a hundred people out to a well-known restaurant to celebrate a child's marriage, is tremendously aggrandizing. Face is why a Chinese who can ill afford to do so may make a grab for a check at an expensive restaurant, and why most Chinese are appalled when Westerners in a group divide up a check. For a Chinese, this would amount to a colossal loss of *mianzi*.

And good luck also brings face. When a Beijing taxi driver rolls down his window to broadcast to all the other drivers in the queue that he has lucked out because the passenger who just got into the cab wants to go all the way out to the airport, he is seeking acknowledgment of the *mianzi* he has just acquired through his good fortune.

Concern for *mianzi* tends to be something Chinese people report about others; it is seldom something they admit about themselves. When I put this conundrum to a Chinese friend, he offered an immediate and logical explanation. To acknowledge that one could ever possibly care about something, or be motivated to do something, based purely on face would be—you guessed it—a tremendous loss of face.

RECAP: NINE POINTS ON FACE

1. Although it is an abstract concept, *mianzi* (face) is deadly serious business to the Chinese. *Mianzi*, money, and power are the three key motivators in China today.
2. A public insult, chastisement, or similar affront to personal dignity results in a loss of face. But in simply contradicting someone in front of another, or declining an invitation on a weak pretext, face may also be lost. Even

the simple act of saying no to a request can be an assault on *mianzi*, which is why Chinese often label things "inconvenient" or "difficult" rather than rejecting them out of hand.

3. Losing control of yourself in any way—whether anger, grief, angst, or any other emotion gets the better of you—always constitutes serious damage to *mianzi*. This includes drinking alcohol to the point of losing self-control.
4. Rescinding an order can also be construed as a loss of face, which is why Chinese leaders may cling adamantly to policies, even when subsequent events prove them irrelevant or misguided. For a leader to change his or her mind is to appear to succumb to pressure or to admit error, both of which involve losing face.
5. Losing face is justification for retaliation. The price exacted may be as low as an apology or as high as a corresponding loss of face on the other side.
6. Organizations have face, too. Ministries, corporations, and bureaus all have reputations to worry about; so do entire countries. Jingoism in China today is strong enough to color the Chinese view of nearly any situation involving foreigners, whether justified or not, and assaults on face may be detected where they are not intended.
7. Chinese spend far more time thinking about face, and see its relevance in far more situations, than foreigners do. Chinese can be counted on to view their human interactions through the lens of face; each and every one represents an opportunity to give, receive, save, or lose *mianzi*.

8. Things that make others look up to you, or be envious of you, also confer face on you. Things that build the ego give face. Doing a favor for a stranger who is introduced to you by a close friend confers *mianzi* on the introducer. Praising someone to his or her boss is also face-enhancing.
9. Face is so important that it is justification for spending money even if a Chinese has little of it. Money that might be set aside for a rainy day or spent on something functional may instead be used to purchase designer clothing and accessories, or to entertain at expensive restaurants.

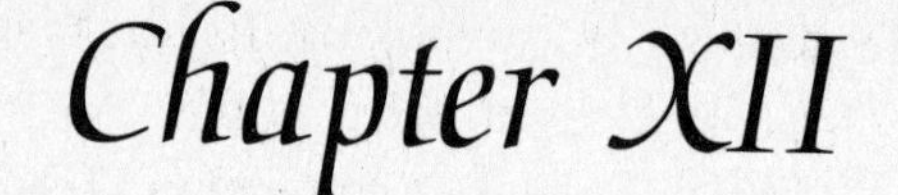

Chapter XII

Getting Things Done in China

LEARNING HOW TO GET THINGS ACCOMPLISHED IN THE PRC is no easy task for a foreigner. The workings of the Chinese system often seem patently irrational to Westerners, though they do possess an internal logic of their own. An appreciation of how things work and why they happen as they do is the key to manipulating the system to serve your ends.

This understanding requires the grasp of several basic points about the Chinese system:

- China's bureaucracy is vast, powerful, entrenched, and exceptionally resistant to change. It is also no monolith, but rather a collection of commissions, ministries, bureaus, and state-owned corporations with their own, often conflicting, bureaucratic interests.
- China still allocates resources in ways that are not necessarily immediately apparent, let alone fair or equitable.

- Where there is a roadblock or what appears to be a no-win situation, the Chinese will usually try to find an indirect solution through which everyone can win.
- The Chinese abhor open conflict among people, so disputes and animosities are either expected to be resolved in peaceful ways or are permitted to fester, quietly unresolved, for years. Either way, preserving decorum and harmony is always of paramount importance.
- The motives that people have for doing things in China include self-aggrandizement, usually in the form of enhancement of face or prestige (see Chapter 11) and financial gain, as well as avoidance of blame, avoidance of responsibility, or simply reduction of one's level of irritation.

THE BUREAUCRACY: MANY CHECKS, FEW BALANCES

Because of the PRC's socialist system, many tasks that would be accomplished in the private sector in a non-Communist nation—such as the manufacture of goods, the provision of housing, or the operation of transportation systems—have traditionally been under the aegis of some unit or other of the government. This has changed rather dramatically over the last decade, as state-owned corporations and, increasingly, even private companies, have assumed many of these functions in the evolving "socialist market economy."

Market forces are increasingly being used to regulate aspects of life formerly controlled by the government, and where the transition has been made, the results have generally been positive. As government control over the country's industry and commerce has declined, so too has its authority over the personal lives of the Chinese people. There is no more government rationing of scarce commodities—indeed, there is far less scarcity; changing jobs is relatively easy to do, ownership of homes and cars is no longer unheard of; and there are even nascent real estate and stock markets.

Traditionally, however, central planning dictated that power be concentrated in Beijing, where dozens of commissions, ministries, administrations, associations, and agencies planned and coordinated the work of the country, and most of these organizations still exist in one form or another. A typical ministry or commission breaks out into many bureaus and divisions. Provincial and municipal governments mirror the structure of the central government. And even in many government-run corporations, the word "government" is often more the operative term than the word "corporation" as far as behavior is concerned.

The chain of command among government units has always been a Byzantine system of dual reporting. For example, a drug factory or corporation located in Shanghai would likely report to the Shanghai Pharmaceuticals Bureau, an organization that itself reports to both the State Pharmaceutical Administration, which is a part of the central government in Beijing, and to the Shanghai municipal government. And various other agencies—the local labor bureau, the local environmental bureau, the local supplies bureau, the local planning bureau, and the local bureau for administration and commerce, to name just a few—would also have regulatory authority over certain activities of the factory.

Innovation in such a huge bureaucracy is bound to be a painful process even when everything runs smoothly—and there is hardly ever a time when everything runs smoothly. There are countless ways to derail a new idea and nearly always someone or some organization with a vested interest in the status quo who has both a say in the decision and a motive to scuttle it. One old saw has it that there are a hundred Chinese bureaucrats empowered to say no for every one who can say yes. There are relatively few ways short of consensus—notoriously difficult to obtain without extensive *guanxi*—to accomplish something novel. To make matters even more difficult, decisions are still sometimes made for political reasons or reasons of *guanxi* instead of economic ones.

Another reason that government decision-making may be perverted is, of course, corruption. Officials make decisions based on many factors, but basic ones are generally what is best for the country and the Chinese people, what is best for their particular ministry, or what is best for themselves personally.

This latter consideration may be expressed in as benign a way as an official's choosing a course of action that will make him or her look good, or as malignant a way as doing what will line his or her pockets. A friend of mine who had received a favor from a government official decided to say thanks not long ago by bringing him a box of chocolate candy. When she presented it to him, he casually let it be known that someone else he had helped recently had given him a Mercedes Benz.

BUREAUCRATIC DECISION-MAKING

The areas controlled by the bureaucracy are vast, and the numbers of people involved phenomenal. Yet it would be hard to imagine a more conservative, change-resistant system. Decisions are most often made by consensus, and they are generally top-down affairs. Since authority is not explicitly delegated to those at lower levels in China, subordinates tend to be insecure about deciding much of anything. You seldom go wrong or are criticized for doing nothing; you are blamed only when you demonstrate initiative. The result is that even the most minor matters are referred up the chain of command, and that the highest-ranking cadres are inundated with minutiae. No one wants to be held accountable for anything.

Then, too, there is the factor that a bad order, once issued, is rescinded only with the greatest of difficulty. As noted in Chapter 11, face is considered to be at stake when someone must go back on a decision. This means that when an official has made a bad policy call, subordinates are loath to approach him or her about changing it, and its chances of remaining in force, no matter how misguided, inconvenient, or destructive it is, are pretty good.

Decision-making can occasionally be fairly expedient, but is more often painfully inefficient and complex. An order by a high-level official is easily executed, for no one would presume to argue with a high-level approval—provided, of course, that it is an official with some authority over you or your organization. But if a decision requires cooperation among more than one unit in the bureaucracy—or even, often, among different departments within the same unit—look out! "Lack of coordination" is only the mildest way to describe what happens.

You should never assume that different departments are sharing information, even when they are supposed to be doing this, or that the information they do share is transmitted accurately. Consider it your responsibility to cover all the bases yourself, and you'll have fewer problems all around.

You can always assume that different units have different interests and that they act in their own interests; you can safely assume most of the time that they do not communicate efficiently with each other. You can frequently assume that there is rivalry among units that share authority over a particular issue, and that they probably dislike one another, making cooperation among them more of an exception than a rule. The only way to get out of a deadlock in which one organization in the bureaucracy is at odds with another is to find a way for both to win or to appeal to an authority superior to both of them. It is often only at this level that a binding decision can be made.

The amount of red tape necessary to accomplish even something very minor can be staggering, and reasons can always be found to foil any request. Precedent is a common one: "We've never had such a request before" often means that we are not interested in entertaining such a request now. Equity is another: "If we make an exception and let you do this, we would have to let everyone do it." And then there are the old standbys: "It is inconvenient to do as you wish" and "Your request is under consideration."

ON THE FRONT LINES

While the titans slug out the policy debates, average bureaucrats still need to get on with their business. They, too, are generally slow to move. But there are many ways to get them not necessarily to change policy, but at least to be more responsive to your particular needs.

Average government functionaries stick their necks out only with great caution, for there is generally little reward for doing so. There is no great face to be had in being innovative or permissive unless one is sure of success, and while there can sometimes be financial gain (in the form of illegal gratuities or favors), there can also be danger if this is discovered. The tried-and-true conservative tack is to avoid accepting responsibility, lest one's decision be construed as the wrong one and one be made to suffer for it later. So an official is likely to be very discouraging when approached with an out-of-the-ordinary request, especially when this request comes from a foreigner.

Then, too, sometimes you encounter resistance from Chinese people not so much for bureaucratic reasons as for personal ones. The individual may not like you or your organization, or may harbor resentment against foreigners in general. Or something in your manner—often the brazen assertiveness that characterizes many Westerners—may have put the person off. The Chinese may not be particularly adept at venting anger, but they can do a masterful job of passive resistance. It's just as effective a way to strike back, and better in that it can be accomplished with a smile.

And finally, people may be less than enthusiastic about helping you get something accomplished due to nothing other than a lack of incentive to do otherwise. Why work hard when there is nothing to be gained? The socialist system in China unfortunately went a long way toward suppressing industriousness. Laziness has been raised to a high art in some government departments, and in some cases it has gotten even worse in the new, incentive-driven China. If everyone else seems to have jumped into the private sector and is working hard and making big money there, why should I exert myself when whatever I do, I still make the same paltry salary in my civil service job?

The reward system in People's China has for decades had little or nothing to do with the amount of effort expended; salaries remained constant whether work was good or bad, productivity high or low. The Chinese call it the *tie fanwan*—"iron rice bowl"—system, an image that makes sense when you understand that one's rice bowl is a traditional symbol for one's livelihood in China, and that to break someone's rice bowl is to deprive that person of his or her means of support. An iron rice bowl is unbreakable, a metaphor for lifetime tenure in a job, regardless of performance.

The iron rice bowl system is gradually being replaced by one that includes bonuses and cash incentives, and many state-owned enterprises have officially embraced "serve the people" and "customer-is-king" ideologies. Old attitudes, however, die hard.

TACTICS FOR "GETTING TO YES"

Nothing is easy in China, but little is impossible. Many tasks that appear undoable can in fact be achieved if you take the proper approach. Just about anything can be negotiated in the PRC, and there are a great many things that must be. Here are some tactics that have worked for others:

Find a win-win solution. A favorite Chinese way to overcome resistance is to identify or create a solution in which either everyone wins, or at least everyone saves face. A good example is a foreign company that ran afoul of one of the government organizations that regulated its activities in China—in this case, an organization responsible for testing the quality of its products. The testing organization regularly found fault with the company's product quality, and was often citing the foreign corporation for violations and fining it accordingly. The foreign company did not agree with the assessment and felt it was being victimized by an activist regulator that saw the company more as a deep pocket than anything else.

After several run-ins with the testing infrastructure, the company got smart. To "improve the accuracy of testing," it underwrote a donation of modern testing equipment—far more up-to-date than what the government had been using. And the problem went away. Whether it was because the new equipment gave a more accurate picture of product quality or because the recipient of a gift is less likely to bite the hand that feeds it is not really knowable, and in any case is not really the point. This company devised a win-win situation that solved not only its own problem, but that of its adversary.

Finding a win-win solution often involves the expenditure of a great deal of effort to uncover the underlying motivation of the organization with which you are struggling, or the person with whom you are dealing. For example, bureaucrats may simply be trying to do their jobs professionally and make decisions based on their particular mandate. Or they may be looking to increase the power and influence of their own organization. Then, too, their motivations may be more personal: face, power, money, or the avoidance of blame, shame, or responsibility.

The twin keys to finding a workable solution are to have as full as possible an understanding of the problem, and also to identify—and accommodate—all of the stakeholders and their motives for action. Getting these often requires a behind-the-scenes inquiry between a trusted Chinese friend and someone in the bureaucracy—in other words, the discreet use of *guanxi*.

Appeal to a higher authority. Another effective, but less preferable, method to get your way when you encounter resistance is to appeal to someone higher up in the chain of command, assuming you can gain access to such a person. If you are in a store or at a ticket counter, you can ask to speak with the manager, and you may or may not be successful. The trick is to find someone who is willing to make a decision and to take responsibility for it.

While such an action might easily earn you the enmity of the underling in the West, under certain circumstances it may actually be appreciated in China. If you make a subordinate look bad in the process, you will of course make yourself an enemy. But if the problem is not that the person does not want to help you, but rather that the person does not believe he or she is empowered to do so, this tactic can do the trick. If a higher-up is willing to overrule a regulation and be accountable for an action, the weight of the decision has been taken off the subordinate's back, and he or she is free to help you out.

Show the proper degree of respect. Nothing fails more assuredly in China than signaling to someone that you do not respect him or her or the job he or she holds. Treating someone like a low-level functionary or petty bureaucrat is a tried-and-true recipe for being turned down, turned away, refused, ignored, or sabotaged. In this respect China is no different from anyplace else, but people in China have a higher than average need for *mianzi*.

When Chinese people interact with authority figures, their default demeanor is typically respectful, deferential, and obedient, if not positively sycophantic. Behavior may even border on the unctuous, and abject toadying is not uncommon. The motive for this sort of behavior may be as much fear of the arbitrary exercise of authority—as in the police officer who might fine you not because you broke the law but because he or she is in a bad mood that day—as it may be the desire for a positive result, such as the answer to a question or the processing of a document.

Following the Chinese lead in this area is often a very effective tactic. People are much more likely to do your bidding in China if you give them the face they feel they so richly deserve.

Catch flies with honey, not vinegar. There is one school of thought that holds that the best way to get what you want from a Chinese service person is to make yourself as obnoxious as you can so that the person is motivated to mollify you just to get you to go away. Over the years I have found, to the contrary, that I am far more likely to be successful if I am friendly than if I am nasty.

This doesn't necessarily mean being compliant and docile; if you are convinced what you are asking for is feasible and ought not to pose major problems, you probably should try pressing your point quietly, calmly, and relentlessly. But not acrimoniously. There is seldom a need for this, and it generally backfires. Remember that the Chinese themselves try to avoid expressing negative emotions as much as they can; to lose your cool is to lose face, and there is little as unforgivable as this.

If you refuse to go away, you may be causing the person more of a problem by making a pest of yourself than satisfying your request would cause. This, however, can be a double-edged sword. You may increase your chances of successful resolution by making it in his or her interest to do what you wish, but you risk getting the person's back up, and if this happens, you are not likely to walk away satisfied. If you choose this tack, in my view it is best accomplished with a smile on your face and even a bit of overt sympathy for the person with whom you are dealing. Remember, he or she might be perfectly willing to help you out, but feel constrained by a regulation or an order from the boss.

Ask the right question. Sometimes getting something accomplished may merely be a matter of communicating more effectively. A Chinese may not fully understand a point you are making, but for reasons of face may be unwilling to admit that this is the case. Or a Chinese may not fully appreciate why you are making a request, and may inadvertently withhold a key piece of information simply because he or she doesn't see it as relevant.

I once spent a full hour at a Chinese post office trying to make arrangements to send a package to the United States. Only after the clerk—who in fact was very accommodating and eager to help—had gone through two different mailing boxes (one was too large for international mail; a second was too heavy and added too much to the postage) and I inquired specifically if there wasn't another way of mailing the item did it dawn on her that using a burlap sack—which was available for sale right at her counter in the post office, and which was cheaper than either of the boxes we had tried—would solve the problem and save me money in the process.

Try the indirect approach. Not only does speaking in soft tones generally get you a great deal further with the Chinese than shrill complaining; it's often a good idea to speak less directly than you might otherwise prefer, and to imply things rather than state them outright. The Chinese themselves frequently give only subtle signals as to their desires. This lack of directness can sometimes be infuriating, but hearing between their words is a skill worth developing. For example, if, during a discussion about a trip to the airport to meet a relative a Chinese asks you whether you have a car, chances are good that he or she would appreciate it if you would offer a ride.

The beauty of such unstated requests is that no face is ever lost as a result of them. Since no request has actually been made, no rebuff has taken place when someone else fails to rise to the bait and make an offer of assistance. No real harm is done if you don't offer to take the trip to the airport. The only problem here arises when these signals are missed entirely by literal-minded Westerners.

A tried-and-true indirect method is to use an intermediary to do your negotiating. The Chinese do this all the time. It permits the flotation of trial balloons and the discussion of sensitive topics that they would find hard to talk about face-to-face (see below).

Offer a way out. When you go head-to-head with a Chinese, one of the most important things to keep in mind is always to offer the person a way out. If you maneuver a person into a corner, you can absolutely count on strong resistance. If, for example, someone tells you that something you wish to buy has been sold out for a week and you confront the person with evidence that he has lied to you—such as the fact that someone you know bought the item there that very morning—don't expect the reaction to be embarrassment and subsequent cooperation.

You may invoke the former, but in putting the person's honor—that is, his face—at stake, you'll get anything *but* the latter. Far better to suggest that perhaps if the person looks in the storage room a second time he or she may discover another box of the items in question that no one had realized was in there.

One way of offering a way out is to use an intermediary, especially when you are in the position of having to deliver bad news to a Chinese. Relaying the message in this way spares the face of the injured party, who may be shocked, furious, hurt, or otherwise distressed. It's important to realize that using an intermediary is not considered a coward's way out in China; among the Chinese there is no premium on confrontation. Conveying bad news through a go-between is generally a desirable method that is easier on everyone.

Don't lose patience. In the majority of cases, when you go up against the Chinese bureaucracy, time is not, or appears not to be, on your side. Urgency can be your worst enemy in trying to get something accomplished, because it can make you willing to pay more and settle for less. China's bureaucracy makes changes grudgingly, and almost never expeditiously. Be prepared to wait and to go over familiar ground several times. Never lose your cool.

Be willing to take risks. You may well want to do something that falls into a gray area as far as the law is concerned. A great deal in China that is worth doing does.

Operating in a gray area carries all the obvious attendant risks. Westerners, as a rule, prefer total clarity, and are used to operating in environments in which it is available. Chinese, on the other hand, may benefit from lack of clarity, and a lot of money can be made at the margins. The authorities are often in no great hurry to clarify gray areas, especially when their friends—or even they themselves—may profit from the ambiguity. They may wink at such areas unless or until they are forced to intervene.

A friend of mine has observed that it's easier to ask forgiveness in China than it is to ask permission, and this is certainly true in a nation in which bureaucrats shy away from taking responsibility for innovation of any kind.

Go through the back door. Knowing people in high—or simply strategic—places, and motivating them to help you out, are important tools. Chinese frequently cultivate such people against the future possibility that a favor will be needed. Examples are endless, but one that comes to mind is a foreign couple who lived in Beijing and were attempting to adopt a Chinese baby. This process is generally a lengthy one because it involves getting approvals from two feuding ministries.

Rather than wait the full year that the adoption agency told them would be required, the couple assiduously cultivated some officials at the ministries in question, befriending them, entertaining them, and doing favors for them. They then exploited these relationships to "jump the queue," and ultimately acquired their baby nearly a half a year before the agency had said they would.

Using *guanxi* to obtain personal favors, services, or goods for which you might not otherwise qualify has a special name in China: to do so is to *zou houmen*, or "go through the back door." When someone uses the powers of his or her office, or even those of a network of friends, to deliver personal favors, this constitutes a use of the back door. Its employment is ubiquitous in the PRC, precisely because many things cannot be accomplished in any other way. The Chinese, accustomed to dealing with organizations in which the front door may merely be a facade, rely on this technique to great effect.

Naturally, access to the back door is not without its costs. People can be motivated in many ways: There are always reciprocal obligations, and there may also be gratuities involved. Someone might be delighted to pull a string to help you get an apartment in a new high-rise building, for example, if you can scare up a Japanese-made refrigerator in return. Or the price might be a *hongbao*, literally a "red envelope," which is expected to contain a certain amount of cash. In China's back-door economy, money, power, and access can all fetch a great deal in return.

GRAFT

One way that many things get accomplished in China—as they do in Taiwan and Hong Kong—is through bribery. Like it or not, there are Chinese, just as there are people in any culture, who accept gratuities for providing hard-to-get and often improper or illegal services. This was only a minor problem in China under orthodox communism, when the stakes were generally quite low, but it has become an unpleasant reality since the opening to the outside world that began in 1979.

This kind of graft is not really in the same category as the relatively innocent gift that someone may give you before asking you to do a favor. In that case you receive the gift before you agree to do anything, and, strictly speaking, the present is not contingent on your willingness to help out. Also, the purpose of such a present may be less to gain your cooperation and more to preserve the face of the giver. It's always bad form to owe someone so much that payback is impossible; a person is not quite as beholden to another if a present has changed hands first.

One hears many stories about a Chinese negotiating team choosing one supplier over another because the deal was sweetened by an overeager foreign company. It might be the inclusion in the deal of an unnecessary but all-expense-paid "fact-finding trip" abroad for the Chinese partner. Or it might be a more brazen act like the delivery of a television set (or, as noted, a Mercedes Benz) to the home of the chief negotiator, or a sum of money to a Swiss or Hong Kong bank account.

I think that many of the stories are exaggerated, but there is no question that this type of activity does go on, especially among the Chinese themselves, and especially in southern China where ties to Hong Kong, Taiwan, and Southeast Asia are closer. Foreign bank accounts in the names of Chinese officials and the transfer of large sums of money to them are without a doubt increasingly commonplace. The scrupulous honesty that invariably characterized PRC businesspeople's dealings with foreigners in the early days of the China trade has, alas, gone the way of Chairman Mao's little red book.

This doesn't in any way imply that you won't run into principled Chinese government officials or businesspeople who will not accept bribes. Lots of PRC officials keep their noses very clean, especially older cadres who are still motivated by socialist ideals. What it does mean is that graft is one of the many currencies that gets wheels turning in China, and that it is one that has been on the ascendancy.

If a Chinese is interested in some sort of payoff, he or she will undoubtedly find some way to let you know. The signal may be a subtle one, but if you are alert for it you can usually pick it up. Alternatively, it might come via an intermediary. You need feel little compunction about turning down such a request, however. Simply explaining that such acts are strictly illegal in your country and that to engage in them would subject you to severe punishment at home can often do the trick. The truth is, they are probably illegal in China as well. The best way to avoid being asked in the first place is to make sure your company has a consistent, well-articulated, well-understood, and well-enforced policy about business ethics, and a strong reputation for probity.

RECAP: SEVEN TIPS ON GETTING THINGS DONE

1. Innovation in China's huge bureaucracy is a painful process. New ideas are often derailed and individuals and organizations with vested interests in the status quo may both have a say in a decision on an innovation and a motive to scuttle it.

2. Officials generally make decisions based on what is best for the country, what is best for their ministry, or what is best for themselves personally. Personal motives may include self-aggrandizement, financial gain, powermongering, avoidance of blame, avoidance of responsibility, and reduction in one's level of irritation.
3. Since authority is not explicitly delegated to them, subordinates tend to be insecure about deciding anything. Even the most minor matters may be referred up the chain of command, and the highest-ranking officials may be inundated with minutiae.
4. There is little reward for a bureaucrat to stick his or her neck out. The conservative tack is to avoid responsibility, lest one suffer for a decision later. Resistance may be for bureaucratic or for personal reasons. The "iron rice bowl" system of lifetime tenure in a job, regardless of performance, has been a real obstacle, but it is disappearing.
5. Tactics for "getting to yes" include:

   - *finding a win-win solution* that solves not only your own problem, but that of your adversary
   - *appealing to a higher authority* willing to make a decision and take responsibility for it
   - *showing respect* and being deferential, obedient, and even a bit sycophantic
   - *catching flies with honey, not vinegar*—keeping interactions friendly rather than nasty
   - *asking the right question*, which means improving communication and making sure you are understood correctly

- *trying an indirect approach* and being subtle when the straightforward approach may lead to loss of face
- *offering a way out* so as to avoid cornering a Chinese in a potentially face-losing situation
- *remaining patient* and not permitting time to work against you
- *being willing to take risks*, recognizing that it's easier to ask forgiveness in China than it is to ask permission
- *going through the back door* by cultivating people in strategic places and motivating them to help you

6. Graft was almost unheard-of in China under orthodox communism, but it is now an unpleasant reality. You will still run into principled Chinese government officials, but corruption is definitely on the ascendancy.
7. If a Chinese is interested in some sort of payoff, he or she will undoubtedly find a way to let you know—a subtle signal or a message through an intermediary. You need feel no compunction about turning down such a request, however. Explain that such acts are illegal in your country and that to engage in them would subject you to severe punishment.

Chapter XIII

Hosting the Chinese

IN MANY BUSINESS RELATIONSHIPS WITH CHINESE ORGANIZATIONS, a company can expect sooner or later to find itself in the position of playing host to a delegation, and of making decisions on requests to host many more. Delegation trips to other countries are Chinese units' favorite methods for assessing foreign technology—and they are real plums for deserving (and not-so-deserving) officials who have little opportunity to travel abroad.

Companies should select carefully, and host only those delegations likely to be important to their business interests in China. The decision should not be made lightly; hosting may mean a great deal of work, may carry many responsibilities, and may be costly in terms of both time and money. And doing it poorly or halfheartedly carries a real risk of causing offense. Once the decision to host is made, there are a number of points to which companies should pay attention, both to make the visit a substantive success and to make sure that the relationships are handled properly and, ideally, deepened as a result of the trip.

Much of the protocol discussed in the previous chapters is equally applicable to dealing with Chinese people both in China and abroad. You'll never go far wrong if you choose to cater to Chinese sensibilities in such areas as meeting and greeting, dining, and conducting business meetings. On the other hand, the Chinese expect things to be different when they travel abroad. You should never feel compelled to discard your own ways simply to make a Chinese more comfortable. There's a difference between taking Chinese customs into account to make someone's stay more enjoyable and slavishly following their rule book and abandoning your own cultural values in the process. If you do the latter, your unease with the situation will be immediately clear, and the entire visit will probably be not only less comfortable, but also less effective all around.

SHOULD YOU HOST A DELEGATION?

Chinese groups travel abroad for many different reasons. A delegation might be a high-level mission headed by a vice premier or minister looking to sign a protocol with the host government, make a sizable purchase, or visit certain facilities of a large company. It might also be a survey group, looking around to see what type of equipment or technology is available but not empowered to sign contracts. Such groups frequently travel abroad to attend conventions or exhibitions, and often attempt to schedule company visits on the side.

On the other hand, the trip could be little more than a ceremonial visit—a reward to some high-ranking cadre about to retire for his or her years of service to a ministry. Or it might be a planning group, eager to assess—or copy—available technology so as to incorporate its acquisition into the country's or the province's five-year plan. It could also be a buying or selling group, willing and empowered to negotiate contracts.

Delegations need not be large, and they need not be formal. While ten to twelve people is probably the norm, they can be as small as half that size. While those led by high-ranking government officials will require a certain amount of protocol, smaller groups are less formal affairs all around, and are, of course, more easily managed.

It is vitally important to know something of a group's composition, its goals, and its authority before you decide whether or not to play host, since hosting carries with it a set of responsibilities (see below). Companies are often approached by far more Chinese delegations than they could ever possibly receive; some say that if they agreed to meet with every group that requests a visit they would do nothing other than host delegations from China.

It's usually fairly clear from a glance at the name list and the answers to a few basic questions whether a given group has a legitimate business interest in asking for a meeting, or whether it is simply trying to fill time to justify staying abroad for an extra day or two. One Los Angeles–based company, to its dismay, came to the conclusion that a Chinese delegation seeking a meeting was interested less in the firm's technology than in whether the company would underwrite a day's excursion for the group to Disneyland.

On the other hand, not every group worth hosting travels with check in hand. Certain survey and planning delegations may not be empowered to contract for purchases, but may have a great deal to say about what technology China should choose when it is time to buy.

Bear in mind that hosting a group may imply a commitment for visits to a half dozen of your company's manufacturing plants over a period of a week or two, or it may simply require making arrangements for a half-day trip to corporate headquarters. The amount of time a company devotes to a group is often negotiable, and should be decided and made clear as early as possible.

THE DELEGATES

A delegation, even if it is composed of individuals from many different Chinese units, functions in essence as if it were a unit unto itself. It has a mandate—perhaps more than one—and a definite structure and hierarchy. Delegations are organized according to a clear rank order, and the individuals in them may hold many specialized functions.

Hosts can generally count on receiving a delegation name list in advance of the visit. Years ago, every Chinese delegation traveled with a complete printed name list that was presented to each host along the way. This custom went out of style as individual name cards became popular in the PRC, but you still occasionally see them. The lists enumerate the delegates in order of protocol, giving their titles and the rank in the delegation of the top few members. If you are asked to host a group and you do not automatically receive a name list before the visit, by all means ask for one; it can help you to decide whether it's a delegation worth receiving or not.

Every delegation has a leader, called a *tuanzhang*. He or she makes major decisions and speaks for the group in all matters. The leader may be supported by a deputy leader, called a *futuanzhang*. If the delegation ever splits up into two groups to attend separate functions, this person generally becomes the head of the splinter group. Senior cadres who may be along on the trip for specific purposes may be designated as advisors, or *guwen*. They hold high rank in the delegation, but generally have no administrative responsibilities; for many the delegation trip is little more than a well-earned boondoggle in advance of retirement.

Beyond these officers, delegations may have secretaries (responsible for taking notes), treasurers (keeping accounts and handling money for the group), interpreters, and liaison officers, who often handle one of the other functions as well. There are almost always one or two very low-ranking individuals who tend to administrative tasks such as collecting luggage at each stop and keeping charge of the group's passports and airline tickets. Very high-ranking groups may also be escorted by a functionary from a Chinese embassy or consulate who is posted in the host country. This person's rank in the delegation can be gauged from his or her position in the delegation name list.

The delegation leader is usually an official from a Chinese government unit or corporation; the delegates themselves may be technicians or engineers. They can usually be counted on to have done their homework and to understand a good deal of the basic technology underlying any given area of interest. At the very least they will be up on contemporary literature in the field, and will have some level of familiarity with your company's products. So it's generally a mistake to underestimate their level of expertise.

DUTIES OF THE HOST

In China, there is a whole set of responsibilities associated with hosting a delegation from abroad, though the list is shrinking as time goes on. In the past, no foreigners were ever permitted in the PRC unless a government unit was willing to take responsibility for them during the visit. The routine tasks shouldered by the *jiedai danwei* (host unit) included authorizing the visa, booking hotel rooms, and arranging site visits and any travel within China. In fact, no Chinese embassy or consulate would even issue a visa without documentation from a host unit in China.

Hosting traditionally also carried with it the burden of running interference for the foreign guest with any other units in China—everything from setting up meetings to mediating disputes, especially if a foreign guest did something wrong or got into any trouble in China, such as having an accident.

China has evolved to the point that one no longer needs a host unit for most purposes. You can get a visa pretty much on demand—though business visas are still harder to get than tourist visas—you can make your own travel and hotel arrangements, and you can make most appointments on your own in China today. The principal thing that remains quite difficult to do on your own recognizance is to arrange appointments with very senior Chinese leaders; for this a host is still generally required.

The Chinese, as usual, extrapolate from their own system. Since making travel and other logistical arrangements in the PRC has always been such a cumbersome process for foreigners (and, for that matter, for locals), many Chinese assume that it will be equally difficult to get around in other countries.

For this reason, and in order to fulfill certain official requirements—like those of foreign embassies that insist on sponsors before they will grant visas, or of Chinese government agencies that demand them before they will authorize passports—they still often seek out hosts in the countries they visit. What these hosts are expected to do can vary greatly and can be negotiated, but many visiting Chinese would like them to do as much as possible of the grunt work involved in setting up their visits.

Sometimes the Chinese use multiple hosts when their trips involve visits to more than one city. A delegation may ask one company or one government agency to act as its national sponsor, or it might appeal to different organizations to make arrangements for it as it travels to different cities. Sometimes, however, it may confuse the picture and ask several companies to arrange the same visit. Naturally, with any given trip it's important to know how arrangements are being handled. The cardinal rule of hosting: Always clarify exactly what is expected of you if you agree to serve as host.

The casual reader might be surprised at how frequently this rule is ignored. Often companies don't focus on the specific demands of their guests until a week or so before the delegation is due to arrive. They may assume their responsibilities begin with receiving the delegation at their facilities and end with seeing them back to the hotel, whereas the Chinese might have something very different in mind. Expectations might include helping them apply for visas, applying pressure to your own country's embassy or consulate in China to expedite the issuance of visas, scheduling audiences with government agencies, setting up meetings with other companies, arranging for the group to be met at each airport and escorted to the hotel in each city, paying for meals, and handling local transportation to each site visited. They may extend to arrangements for shopping, sight-seeing, and other leisure time activities and even to per diem allowances for expenses.

It's worth bearing in mind as you consider the level of hospitality you intend to provide that most Chinese government and private organizations have their own cars and entertainment budgets—they may even own their own dining establishments. It is hardly any effort for them to offer these amenities to visitors to China, so they often feel justified in expecting the same courtesies when they travel abroad.

It is also worth considering the fact that any given Chinese delegation may also be approaching your competitors at the same time that your company is being asked for help. The Chinese can be counted on to remember courtesies extended to them when they are abroad—as well as those that are notable in their absence.

You may not feel comfortable raising with the Chinese specific issues relating to the extent of the hospitality you are prepared to provide, for fear of appearing less than gracious should you decline to go to the trouble or expense of fulfilling all the delegation's desires. But it is very important to do so. Only if responsibilities are clearly defined can you be certain that there will be no misunderstandings. Far better to have a moment of unease during the negotiating stage than a major snafu when a delegation gets stranded at an airport or caught without sufficient funds to pay a hotel bill.

Companies that host Chinese technical delegations for months at a time often run into a whole additional set of problems. In such situations the Chinese groups need to have their housing, transportation, and entertainment needs addressed.

Since delegates frequently do not speak English and do not hold driver's licenses, hospitality sometimes requires assigning a company staff member—ideally one who can speak some Chinese—to see to their comfort.

Accommodations

Sometimes Chinese and foreign counterparts reach reciprocal hospitality agreements whereby the visitor picks up the tab for international travel, but the host bears responsibility for local expenses in the country being visited. Such agreements are good deals for the Chinese, since basic services are cheaper in China. More typically, each side pays its own expenses when it visits the other's country.

If you are charged with making hotel arrangements for a visiting Chinese group that will be responsible for its own local expenses, be sensitive to costs. Many Chinese delegations do not want to spend their own money, which would be necessary for first-class treatment on every leg of their journey. Though high-ranking groups may wish to stay at the best hotels—for reasons of face if nothing else—most delegations are looking for clean, comfortable accommodations at bargain basement rates. If in doubt, be sure that you let the Chinese know in advance how much the hotel charges per room. In fact, tell them how much money to bring along with them for the entire trip, since most Chinese do not carry credit cards.

It's also important to find out whether the norm for the delegation will be single or double rooms, and whether any of the higher-ranking delegates will need suites. It's not important to assign roommates in advance of arrival; the Chinese will do that themselves. Chinese groups often request one suite that is occupied by the delegation leader and is also used for group meetings. If it is an important group and you are picking up the tab, you may want to consider booking a suite for the delegation head; if the Chinese will bear responsibility for local costs, check with them first to see what their wishes are in this regard.

Ask the hotel to accommodate the entire group on one floor, or in one wing, if at all possible. Proximity to an interpreter is important to a hotel guest who cannot communicate in the local language and who may need to deal with hotel staff for such matters as laundry, room service, or long distance telephone calls.

If it is a first trip abroad for many of the delegates, you might consider offering them an informal briefing on safety and security in your country. First-time visitors may not be well equipped to deal with the dangers present in many Western cities, and may need to be reminded of a few basic precautions: to avoid flashing large sums of cash and leaving valuables in hotel rooms, to use travelers' checks, and to safeguard items such as airline tickets.

Certain amenities, while not de rigueur, are very much appreciated, such as meeting a visiting group at the airport or seeing them off when they leave. Other gestures may be offered but are not necessarily required. Transportation for the delegation, for example, may be provided free of charge, or at the group's own expense.

FORMALITIES

Meeting visitors at the point of entry and seeing them off on their departure were traditionally viewed as an official responsibility of the group's principal host, and in the old days such formalities were best not overlooked when receiving high-ranking Chinese guests. Furthermore, the guests had to be received by someone of suitably high rank in the host organization.

This is still the way to go when hosting very high-ranking Chinese, for whom failure to meet and greet may be seen as a gratuitous slight (see Chapter 3). It is also an appropriate gesture when your company wants to signal any Chinese group that it holds them in particularly high esteem or places great importance on their visit. Generally speaking, however, the meeting ritual is far less important today, when groups are less formal and better traveled outside of China. Chinese who have experience with Westerners increasingly understand that this ceremony is simply not customary in other countries.

Make sure whoever greets the group—whether at the airport or the corporate headquarters—is well briefed. Note particularly any members of the delegation that officers or staff of your company have met before. It's quite awkward when a Chinese—or anyone else, for that matter—expects to be remembered and is not. Conversely, it is appreciated when a company president recalls, or even pretends to recall, a previous meeting with a delegate.

If your Chinese visitor is a very high-ranking individual or if you desire for other reasons to receive a Chinese guest in grand style, providing transportation is a good way to signal respect. Often a limousine is furnished for the delegation leader and one or more very high-ranking delegates, with the balance of the group traveling together in another car, a bus, or a minivan. In such situations, the principal host travels together with the Chinese delegation leader and an interpreter, if necessary.

If there are many high-ranking delegates and all cannot fit comfortably into the limousine, a second car may be employed for them.

One caveat here: Some delegations prefer not to be split up, and will happily forgo the special treatment in favor of a minibus that will keep all the delegates in close proximity. If you do arrange a limousine it's a good idea to check in advance and make sure the Chinese wish it; alternatively, remain flexible and be prepared to switch modes of transportation on short notice if you are asked to do so.

Even if your company president can't make it to the airport, scheduling an audience with him or her—or with some other responsible corporate official—is a much-appreciated gesture. To do so is to give face to the Chinese delegation (see Chapter 11) and to signal the visitors that your company takes them and their business seriously.

PLANNING THE SCHEDULE

One of the first activities you should consider scheduling with a visiting group from China is an itinerary meeting. This can be an informal discussion with the delegation's liaison person or interpreter, or it can be a more official session; it depends on the level of formality of the delegation, how well you know the members and whether or not you anticipate that the group will require last-minute changes to the agenda.

The purpose of the meeting is to secure Chinese assent to the arrangements that have been made for them. It is a way of confirming that the itinerary and agenda you have planned are satisfactory. Holding such a meeting decreases the chances of things going awry during the visit, such as an important delegation official's opting not to attend a crucial meeting, or the group's splitting up so that half of them can participate in some activity entirely unrelated to the visit with your company.

The itinerary meeting is also your opportunity to determine whether the delegates plan to do anything else in your city during the time they are visiting with you. By holding the discussion shortly after the delegation's arrival, you have also given yourself time to make adjustments to the schedule if for any reason the arrangements are not acceptable.

Many companies make name badges for Chinese visitors and ask the delegates to wear them so their hosts will know how to address them. Chinese accept these willingly when they are offered. Don't forget, however, that they will need to know what to call their hosts as well, so if you hand out name badges be sure your side wears them, too. The labels should be bilingual if possible.

Distances between China and countries in Europe and North America are great. If the visit to your company is the first stop on the group's U.S. tour, for example, you might want to keep the first day's schedule light to permit the delegates time to overcome jet lag, which is particularly severe after a flight over such a long distance from West to East. Generally the first official gathering is some sort of briefing about the company—an introductory presentation giving basic facts about the company's structure, history, products, production, and sales statistics. Don't worry about boring your guests or even about repeating something most of the delegates already know; you'll probably find them taking copious notes anyway.

Many companies are also asked by the Chinese to arrange

factory tours. Here the technicians and engineers on the delegation can be counted on to ask probing technical questions, and to prepare properly for such visits you should certainly have on hand someone who can answer these. If the answers are proprietary—technological secrets that you wish to sell to the Chinese, are prohibited from revealing or simply do not wish to divulge—be honest and tell your guests why. If there are restrictions on photographing inside the factory, tell them that as well. They can easily accept such limits when they are explained clearly.

The most senior corporate officer who receives a group at the airport or at a banquet need not accompany the group throughout its visit, though the more time he or she makes available, as a rule, the more *mianzi* is conferred on the visitors. It is important, however, that someone of sufficiently high stature stay with the group during its visit—unless of course the delegation will be staying for a period of weeks or months. It's also important to make available someone capable of fielding the technical questions that the Chinese delegates will inevitably have.

You should definitely plan to provide your Chinese guests with materials relevant to their visit. A schedule or itinerary prepared in Chinese will be most welcome, but at very least an English version should be provided. A complete name list of the company officers the guests will be meeting should also be offered.

Technical materials related to the product or technology a Chinese group is interested in buying should also be prepared; again, if you can arrange for these materials to be translated into Chinese, by all means do so. If the group will be staying in your city for a prolonged period of time, literature on how to get around will also be welcome.

Conducting Meetings

When your company first agrees to play host to a visiting group from China, you should do all you can to find out the exact purpose of the group's visit to your country, and the specific goals they hope to accomplish by visiting your organization. Establishing the intentions of the Chinese side and determining your own company's objectives in hosting the group are the most important steps in ensuring a successful visit.

A group may well have many goals, not just one. Various delegates, especially if they work for different units in China, will have divergent interests and will be looking for distinct things. You can often make an educated guess at the area of interest simply by looking at the person's title.

After the goals are clarified, presentations can be outlined accordingly. A coordinator for the visit can make sure the appropriate divisions within the company are represented and given some exposure to the delegation, and that the material they present is responsive to the information needs of the visitors. Once a tentative program has been drawn up, it's advisable to run a copy of it by the Chinese side for their comments, or by their representative if this is easier. The more advance information the Chinese are given, the better prepared they will be, and the more confident you can be that you are on the right track.

Remember in planning presentations that the need for consecutive interpretation means that time allotted must be multiplied by two. If you can prepare a bilingual text outline of what will be discussed, so much the better. Give some thought to interpreters, too. While the Chinese side will bring along its own translator, supplying one from your side is an excellent idea, provided the person is competent. Someone familiar with the Chinese translations for the technical terms of your trade would be ideal. Whoever does the translating should be given an advance text of each presentation, even if it exists only in outline form. A little preparation can make the difference between a rudimentary understanding and a thorough grasp of the material.

Throughout the visit, the Chinese will probably pose many questions. Those that cannot be answered as they are asked should be noted, together with any requests made by the delegates for further information. It's an important show of sincerity to follow up on such requests religiously and to make sure that the guests receive answers, unless of course there is a reason to withhold the information. In that case, it's best to tell the guests why.

COCKTAILS AND DINING

Formal entertaining generally plays a part in hosting delegations. If time permits, it is customary to treat a delegation to lunch or dinner while it is visiting your organization. There is no need to do this more than once or twice, however, even if the group stays with you for a long period of time.

If you plan a luncheon or dinner where Chinese and hosts will be present together, you'll want to assign seats and mark place settings with place cards. This is advisable, if only to avoid the otherwise natural phenomenon of Chinese choosing to sit with other Chinese and Westerners with other Westerners. Since the reason for taking the meal together is presumably for the two sides to get to know each other better, it's important to sprinkle representatives of both sides across all of the tables, and make sure that there are interpreters on hand at each table to facilitate communication.

It's probably best in such situations to follow the rules of Chinese protocol seating (see Chapter 8). You need not do this slavishly, but do try to keep within the spirit if not the letter of protocol order. If you place the principal Chinese guest at table three, far from your company chairman, you're bound to end up with hurt feelings. Similarly, don't put someone at a particular table for social reasons; the fact that your company president enjoyed Mr. Wang's questions during the business meeting is no reason to bump Mr. Wang up five steps in protocol order and seat him at the head table in a seat that would rightfully belong to Mr. Zhou.

As long as you are operating within approximate protocol order, however, it is acceptable to seat people next to each other for substantive reasons. Placing a Chinese and a Western engineer next to each other so that they can discuss technical matters relating to a venture being negotiated is a good idea, and it's perfectly acceptable.

Do escort your guests to their seats. If possible, make sure the place cards are bilingual so the Chinese guests can find their own places, and so the Westerners seated on either side of them can determine who their dining partners are. If the meal is a buffet, the Chinese will need an explicit invitation before they will line up and help themselves.

If you are hosting a dinner, remember that Chinese tend

to eat early, and are generally finished with their meals by about eight o'clock. They don't usually enjoy cocktails or a cocktail hour before dinner. If they are required to wait for an eight o'clock dinner, they may perish from hunger. It is also probably better all around if you avoid hosting the Chinese for excessively formal affairs. Chinese businessmen invariably wear Western suits these days, but few own tuxedos or tails.

PLANNING MENUS

When Chinese people visit other countries, it is not necessary for their hosts to offer Chinese-style banquets in their honor. Just as visitors to China expect the etiquette—not to say the food—to be different in the PRC, the Chinese are aware that in other countries things are done differently. Still, organizing a banquet at a Chinese restaurant is a popular means of entertaining Chinese visitors, and one they very much appreciate. In truth, the Chinese believe their cuisine, with all of its regional variations, is the best in the world. After a week or so of "foreign food," any Chinese delegation will be glad for a taste of home.

If you are planning a Western-style meal you should keep in mind that while well-traveled Chinese will eat just about anything, those who have spent little time outside of China, and those who are from rural areas, may find certain dishes problematical. Here are a few tips on choosing the menu:

First of all, refrain from serving very large chunks of red meat—beef, pork, or anything else—and especially avoid serving steaks that are blood rare or undercooked. Salads consisting of raw vegetables are not high on Chinese wish lists; vegetables are almost always cooked in China. Many Chinese also eschew dairy products such as sour cream and cheese—especially highly aromatic cheeses such as blue cheese.

A Western-style meal that succeeds with the Chinese is more likely to include rice or noodles than bread. It's also more likely to be a buffet than a sit-down dinner, since the former offers a choice of entrees. Dishes made up of small pieces, such as stews and stir-fried vegetables, are very welcome. Make sure vegetables are cooked, though never to the point that they lose their crispness. And poultry and seafood are always appreciated, just so long as they aren't smothered in cream sauces.

Few PRC delegations leave China without rudimentary training in the basics of Western etiquette—how to tie a tie, how to hold a knife and fork, and so on. But expect some lapses in table etiquette, especially if your Chinese guest is from a rural area or is not well educated. This may include talking with a mouth full of food, forgetting to use a napkin, buttering a roll with a fork or spoon, or discarding a bone or a shell on the tablecloth or even the floor.

Amenities and Bugaboos

Listed below are a few special ways in which you can make your Chinese visitors feel very much at home, and a few sensitive areas that you'd be well advised to watch out for:

Snack food and tea. Most Chinese visitors required to eat Western food for any length of time will probably be homesick for a taste of China. A good way to provide some sustenance for the delegates who only pick at their steak and potatoes—and a treat even for those more comfortable with Western cuisine—is to supply your guests with instant noodles and some way to boil water—an inexpensive, plug-in hot pot, for example. A cup of instant noodles before bedtime can really work wonders.

Another favorite snack is fresh fruit. Providing a visiting Chinese with a basket of fruit in his or her room is a most welcome gesture. If you were thinking of fresh flowers, think again; some apples or a bunch of bananas is a much better idea. And a container of loose tea with a thermos of hot water will also be most appreciated; Chinese hotels provide these in each room as a matter of course.

Lightening the load. Delegations that stay abroad for lengthy periods and that visit many different companies or countries may amass mountains of printed materials. If companies provide copies for everyone on the delegation, that's a dozen or so copies of each brochure and pamphlet. An offer to mail the brochures back to China on the delegation's behalf is almost always graciously accepted.

Gift-giving. Most Chinese delegations carry gifts with them to present to each organization that hosts them. You can expect to receive a gift if you entertain a Chinese group. Strictly speaking, it is not necessary to reciprocate, since it is you who are offering hospitality. But a memento of the occasion is always welcome. Giving inexpensive individual gifts—pens, cigarette lighters, briefcases, baseball caps, tape measures, and so on—that show your company's logo is common practice. For more on this, see Chapter 9.

Entertaining at home. It's a real treat for a Chinese to be entertained at the home of a corporate host. Not only is this a personal honor; it's a great way to satisfy curiosity about how the other half lives, and an excellent way to break the ice. If you invite Chinese delegates to your home, it's fine to have your spouse and children on hand. In fact, it's probably expected.

Welcoming signs. One other amenity that is in no way expected or necessary but that is appreciated is a sign welcoming the group at the location to be visited. In order for it to be effective, of course, the sign should be written in Chinese. I once escorted a Chinese delegation to the headquarters of a multinational company where they were greeted by a large banner in Chinese proclaiming the company's enthusiastic welcome. The only glitch was that the banner had been hung upside down. The Chinese were amused by the mishap, but they appreciated the gesture very much nonetheless.

Flags. Some companies also decide to hang the Chinese flag out front as a sign of welcome. This is fine—and much appreciated—so long as you use the right flag. The sensitivity here is to the flag used by Taiwan, which despite loss of recognition by most Western countries still manages to show up in many places.

The PRC flag is red with five stars on it, one larger than the other four. That's the *only* flag to use when hosting mainland groups. Taiwan's "Republic of China" flag also has a red background, but it has a blue field in the upper left-hand corner with one large, white sunlike star on it. Make sure it is well out of sight before a PRC delegation shows up. Mainland groups have been known to turn on their heels in protest and walk right out of a building that displays the Taiwan flag, so this is nothing to be taken lightly.

Maps. In a related vein, something else to watch out for is the use of maps in your sales or corporate literature. Showing Taiwan on any map of China is not only perfectly acceptable, it is required. And be sure Taiwan is not portrayed in any way as an independent country, or as an entity separate from the mainland. Avoid the "Republic of China" label like the plague, and don't show Taiwan in a color different from that of the rest of China.

This should not be problematical when you host groups from Taiwan, by the way. The government of Taiwan also regards Taiwan as a part of China. For Taiwan groups, however, you might wish to stay away from PRC flags. For Hong Kong groups, don't worry; since Hong Kong's reversion to Chinese sovereignty in 1997 they now fly the PRC flag (as well as one of their own) and consider themselves a part of China.

Photography. By all means invite the company photographer out to take some photos of the Chinese visitors. Not only might these be useful for the company newsletter (see below), but they are excellent follow-up gifts for your next trip to China. The Chinese love photographs, and a picture of you and the delegation standing at your company's factory in front of an important piece of equipment is not only a valuable memento; it is also a way to keep your company and its products fresh in your guests' minds for many months.

The Chinese themselves will almost certainly come equipped with cameras. If there is any sensitivity regarding the taking of photos in the facility to be toured, say so; telling the Chinese it is your company's policy to disallow photographs will end the matter then and there. Don't worry about hurt feelings; rules like this are completely understandable to the Chinese. The same regulations apply to sensitive areas, such as military installations, in the PRC.

MEDIA

Visits by important Chinese delegations are often of great interest to local media. Many companies find that when word gets around in the community that a high-ranking Chinese official will be touring their facilities, the local press is eager to cover the story.

With some exceptions, Chinese groups tend to be media-shy. This is especially true when they visit countries with activist media that regularly take the Chinese government to task for violation of human rights, intellectual property rights, unauthorized technology transfer to renegade countries, and other high crimes and misdemeanors. While it is not unheard-of for an occasional Chinese delegation to agree to talk to the media—especially if the group is selling products or attempting to attract foreign investment—the fact remains that most delegations still prefer to keep a low profile.

The rule of thumb here, as elsewhere, is to avoid surprises. If the Chinese agree in advance to receive a journalist, you need not hesitate to arrange an interview. But if you value your company's relationship with the Chinese group, the media should never be forced on them when they are your guests. Getting off an airplane to confront a crowd of belligerent reporters is no Chinese official's idea of a day at the beach.

Don't interpret this warning to mean that it isn't acceptable to cover a Chinese delegation visit in your company's in-house newsletter. It certainly is. Just explain to your guests the purpose of the photo or of the interview, and nine times out of ten you'll get complete cooperation.

RECAP: THIRTEEN WAYS TO BE A GOOD HOST

1. Hosting delegations from China carries many responsibilities and can be costly. Since companies are often approached by far more Chinese delegations than they could ever possibly receive, it's important to choose carefully which ones to host.
2. Delegations have definite structures and hierarchies. The name list enumerates delegates in protocol order, starting with the delegation leader. He or she makes major decisions and speaks for the group in all matters.
3. The Chinese expect hosts to coordinate the trips and generally help things go smoothly. Sometimes more than one host is contacted, confusing things. Always clarify exactly what is expected of you if you agree to serve as host, in order to avoid misunderstandings.
4. The Chinese pay their own expenses unless otherwise stated. Be sensitive to what they can afford, and let them know in advance how much major items cost. Ask the hotel to accommodate the entire group on one floor if

possible; proximity to an interpreter is important. Consider briefing first-time visitors on security precautions.

5. Try to arrange for someone of suitably high rank in your company to meet important visitors at the airport and see them off when they leave. Make sure whoever greets the group is well briefed. Providing transportation is a good way to show hospitality. Schedule an audience with a responsible corporate official if possible.
6. Schedule an itinerary meeting after arrival to secure Chinese assent to the arrangements. Keep the first day's schedule light if necessary to allow guests time to overcome jet lag. Offer a basic briefing about the company. Someone of suitable rank should stay with the group during its visit, unless it is a prolonged stay.
7. Provide Chinese guests with a schedule or itinerary in Chinese or English, as well as a name list of the company officers the guests are to meet. Also distribute technical materials related to the product or technology discussed.
8. Remember the need for consecutive interpretation; time allotted must be multiplied by two. A bilingual text outline of discussion points is appreciated. Note questions that cannot be answered as they are asked, and follow up on them.
9. If you plan a sit-down meal, mark seats with place cards. Follow protocol order in seating. Don't make Chinese guests wait too long to be served, as they normally finish dinner by around eight o'clock.
10. If you are planning a Western-style meal, avoid large chunks of red meat and blood-rare steaks. Raw vegetable salads and dairy products are chancy. Try to serve rice or noodles, stews, or stir-fried vegetables.

11. As a treat, supply your guests with instant noodles, Chinese tea, and a way to boil water; fresh fruit is also welcome. Offer to lighten their load by mailing company brochures back to China. Give inexpensive souvenirs; photos of the delegates visiting your company are excellent mementos.
12. A welcoming sign at the site to be visited is appreciated, as is a display of the Chinese flag, but make sure it is the right flag. Watch out also for any maps that show Taiwan as an entity separate from China.
13. Media should never be forced on the Chinese when they are your guests. If they agree in advance to receive a journalist, don't hesitate to arrange an interview. Feel free to cover a Chinese delegation visit in your company's in-house newspaper.

Afterword

THIS BOOK IS ALL ABOUT BALANCE. ON ONE HAND, IT IS ABOUT understanding and accommodating people with unfamiliar patterns of interaction that may seem, at times, to be gracious, strange, funny, obsequious, indirect, refreshing, counterproductive, and downright maddening. On the other hand, it is also about being yourself: being true to your own cultural traditions and values, and behaving in accordance with the best of these. Such balance is difficult, but your success with the Chinese requires that you strive for it, since you won't achieve much by tilting too far to either side.

No one gets very far in China without at least learning to read the signals. What is *not* said is as important as what *is*, and *how* something is said can speak volumes. Like it or not, the Chinese will never be as straightforward as you might wish, and you're going to have to be alert for subtle signs and patterns if you are to discern the true meaning of their behavior. Taking it at face value may be tempting, but most of the time it's a fairly inaccurate barometer of what's really going on.

Once you've learned to read the subtexts, you have to decide how much you want to play the game. Should you bend over backward to avoid causing Mr. Wang to lose face? Should you try to cultivate a relationship with Ms. Zhou simply to secure her cooperation or approval on a business deal? It's really up to you, but remember that no matter how silly you may feel it is, face is serious business to Mr. Wang. And Ms. Zhou is unlikely to work very hard on behalf of someone who has ignored her.

I freely admit I am no agnostic on this subject. I believe strongly that showing respect for the Chinese point of view is the key to enjoying successful relationships with them. For me, it means finding a private moment if I must criticize someone and choosing words that do not pack a punch. It means actively seeking opportunities to give face and enhance people's prestige. It means going the extra mile to serve food to guests at banquets, being careful during meetings not to seize the floor when it isn't my turn, controlling my anger in public, and looking for win-win solutions to problems, even when I am extremely annoyed at my counterpart for some offense or other.

To a certain extent I do these things for utilitarian reasons: I have learned that I get better results from the Chinese when I do. But another factor is that I have come to see the wisdom in certain aspects of the Chinese approach—ways of doing things that may be kinder, more sensitive, or more polite than my standard American modus operandi would dictate.

My willingness to behave in a Chinese way ends, however, when I feel I am compromising something essential in my own personality, or when I believe my sense of ethics or morality may be in jeopardy. I may choose my moments and my words more carefully, but I don't move mountains to suppress my candor when I am dealing with Chinese friends, nor will I permit myself to become a slave to surface harmony, especially when my inclination is that honesty is a better policy in a given situation.

I am pleased to enter into relationships with Chinese people, not only because I enjoy them intrinsically and learn from them, but also because I need *guanxi* to get things accomplished as much as the next fellow. I do not, however, accept favors out of proportion to what I intend to give, and I refuse to give bribes, break the law, or do anything I believe to be immoral. The truth is, being true to your own essential nature, knowing your own limitations, and drawing your own lines ultimately earn you respect even from Chinese counterparts trying their hardest to get you to do things their way.

Then too, China itself is nothing if not a moving target. You have to travel farther and farther into the countryside these days to find Chinese who are as unaware of Western ways as most were a dozen or more years ago. And many urban Chinese are in fact growing quite sophisticated in their understanding—and, in some cases, imitation—of Western values and standards of behavior. So one can make a strong argument that the gap is, in fact, narrowing of its own accord.

Nonetheless, there are still those inclined to be afraid of China or of the Chinese. Fear of China isn't as silly as it may sound; the very foreignness of the country has persuaded many Westerners over several centuries that China is ultimately inscrutable, and that they can't trust their instincts in a culture governed by such an incomprehensible set of rules of conduct. If this book demonstrates anything it is that many of the rules are essentially the same, that many allowances are made for foreigners who aren't aware of them, and that those rules that are not familiar are nonetheless understandable, even if it isn't always easy to follow them.

The truth is, the Chinese are *not* inscrutable, and dealing with them doesn't require exchanging the contents of your cultural baggage for a new suit of clothes that doesn't fit you. It requires learning when you *can* trust your instincts, which is probably most of the time. But it also requires learning when and how to look more deeply into a situation for a more Chinese interpretation of what's really going on. Finally, to get the results you desire, it sometimes also requires learning to formulate a Chinese-friendly response.

In my book, it's well worth the trouble.

Appendix

A Guide to Chinese Romanization and Phonics

You'll get a lot further in China if you learn to say the names of the people you meet and the places you go properly. The Chinese don't expect foreigners to speak their language, but are tickled when you try. Still, you may have some difficulty being understood without a little guidance. This section provides a basic introduction to Mandarin Chinese phonics that should help you pronounce not only the Chinese terms used in this book, but also the names and other words you'll encounter when you are in China.

Pinyin Romanization

The Chinese terms used in this book are expressed in a romanization system called *pinyin*—a Chinese word meaning nothing more than "spelling." It is one of many systems of phonetic rendering of Chinese, but in the last twenty-five years has become the dominant system on the mainland and in many other parts of the world.

Developed in the 1950s primarily for teaching the language to Chinese children and to foreigners, *pinyin* is the official romanization system of the People's Republic of China. To the extent that you encounter any romanized words there, this is the system of spelling that will probably be used. It became popular in the West in the late 1970s. You'll probably recognize *pinyin* as the system that dictated that the world start referring to the late Teng Hsiao-p'ing as Deng Xiaoping and Peking as Beijing.

Pinyin is based on the phonics of the Mandarin dialect (called *putonghua* on the mainland, *guoyü* in Taiwan, and *huayü* in Southeast Asia and elsewhere). While you may encounter it in Hong Kong as well, it does *not* provide an effective way of romanizing the Cantonese dialect spoken there. Nor will you see it used in Taiwan—where Mandarin in fact is widely spoken—because it is a communist invention. The older Wade-Giles system—which gave us Mao Tse-tung before he was Mao Zedong—is more widespread in Taiwan; other, less common systems are used there as well.

Chinese adults actually have little use for romanization, so don't expect a Chinese person to be very familiar with *pinyin* or any other romanized spelling system. Written Chinese makes use of a system of tens of thousands of characters, or ideograms, that stand for words and contain little or no phonetic information, meaning they must be memorized. Even though China is a land of many dialects, the written language is consistent throughout the mainland, and it includes many characters that are rendered in simplified forms popularized by the communists beginning in the 1950s. In Hong Kong, Macao, Taiwan, and most other parts of the world, these simplified forms were never formally adopted, and Chinese characters are written in their traditional, or standard, forms.

Though it takes many years to learn to read Chinese efficiently, China boasts a very high literacy rate. The Chinese use characters exclusively in their day-to-day lives. For the purposes of the occasional traveler to China, however, a working knowledge of *pinyin* is all you're likely to need to get by.

Pronouncing Chinese

A Chinese word is composed of one or more syllables, each of which is rendered with its own character. And any Chinese syllable can be divided into three components: an initial sound, a final sound, and a tone or intonation. It's the *pinyin* rendering of the initials that gives some Westerners the most trouble, since a few of the conventions adopted are not intuitive to native speakers of English. If you remember a few facts about the four most troublesome letters—that a *q* at the beginning of a word is pronounced like *ch*, an *x* like *sh*, a *c* like *ts* and a *z* like *dz*—you're 85 percent of the way there, since most of the other letters perform pretty much as they do in English. Here's the complete table of *pinyin* initials, together with some approximate equivalent pronunciations in English:

Initials

Pinyin Initial	English Equivalent
b	same as English
c	like the *ts* in "cats"
ch	same as English
d	same as English
f	same as English
g	same as English
h	like an *h* sound, only more guttural; actually more like the *ch* in the German word "ach"
j	like the *j* sound in "Jeep"
k	same as English
l	same as English
m	same as English
n	same as English
p	same as English
q	like the *ch* in China
r	somewhere between the English *r* and *j* sounds; a bit like the *s* sound in "leisure"
s	same as English
sh	same as English
t	same as English
w	same as English
x	like the *sh* in "she"
y	same as English
z	like the *ds* in "buds"
zh	like the *j* sound in "jail"

For the finals, too, your knowledge of English will not generally lead you too far astray, except for a few tricky ones. Below is a complete table of *pinyin* finals with equivalent sounds in English:

Finals

Pinyin Final	English Equivalent
a	like the *a* sound in "Pa"
ai	like the *ie* in "pie"
an	like the word "on"
ang	like the *ong* in "throng"
ao	to rhyme with "cow"
ar	like the *ar* in "bar"
e	like the *oo* in "wood"
ei	like the *a* sound in "say"
en	like the *un* in "bun"
eng	like the *ung* in "sung"
er	like the *er* in "her"
i	like the *e* sound in "me" after the initials b, d, l, m, n, p, q, t, and x; like *z* after c, s, and z; and like *r* after ch, r, sh, and zh
ia	like the *ia* in "Pennsylvania"
ian	like the word "yen"
iang	"yahng," to rhyme with "Hong Kong"
iao	like the *yow* in "yowl"
ie	like the *ye* in "yes"

in	to rhyme with "mean"
ing	like the *ing* in "king"
iong	"yawng," to rhyme with "wrong"
iu	like the word "yo"
o	like the *aw* in "raw"
ong	to rhyme with "wrong"
ou	to rhyme with "hoe"
u	like the *oo* in "boo"
ü	like the German *ü* sound or the French *eu*
uai	like the beginning of the word "wide"
uan	like the word "wen" after j, q, x, and y; like the word "wan" after other letters
uang	like the surname of "Suzie Wong"
ue	like the beginning of the word "wet"
ui	like the word "way"
un	like the word "win" after j, q, and x; to rhyme with "won" after other letters
uo	like the *aw* in "claw"

Chinese syllables are combinations of initials and finals. Thus the word *xiao*, which means "small," is a combination of the initial *x*, pronounced "sh," and the ending *iao*, pronounced "yao." The syllable is thus said "shyao." *Ren*, meaning "person," is a combination of the initial *r* and the final *en*. Some words, like these two examples, are just one syllable long. Other words are combinations of two or more syllables, each the sum of an initial and a final.

TONES

To complete the story, however, you must also understand tones. Chinese is a sound-poor language; that is, combining initials and finals yields a relatively small number of possible pronunciations. The size of this universe is increased, however, since every syllable also has a tone contour, or intonation, in addition to an initial and a final. This means that each syllable must be pronounced in the proper tone of voice in order for one's meaning to be clear. Spoken Mandarin has four such basic tones: a high, even tone; a rising tone; a dipping tone; and a falling tone. It also has a neutral, or nonstressed, tone.

English has intonation patterns, too, but not nearly to the extent that Chinese does. For example, if you pronounce the sentence "The book is on the table" first normally and then with a rising intonation, you can see that by varying only the intonation you can change a declarative sentence into an interrogative one. The difference is that in Chinese, each syllable has a tone, and their various meanings have absolutely nothing to do with one another.

In Chinese, the syllable *tang* can mean "soup" (when said in a high, even tone), "sugar" (a rising tone), "to lie down" (a dipping tone), and "to iron something" (a descending tone). And, depending on the actual character, it can mean a lot of other things as well, such as "a common surname, a hall, a kind of poplar tree, an embankment, a door frame, your chest, to bore, a mantis, the state treasury, to shed," or "an incidence." Most Chinese words have many homonyms, and tones help cut down the number of options, enabling people to understand one another without too much difficulty. Context generally does the rest.

Serious students of the Chinese language must concern themselves with tones; for the casual visitor, however, they may be ignored without sacrificing too much in the way of meaning. To avoid confusion, tone marks have been omitted throughout this book.

*Glossary of Chinese Terms Used in This Book**

ai 爱, "love." One of the eight Confucian virtues.

airen 爱人, mainland Chinese term for "spouse." Also means "lover."

ayi 阿姨, "aunt," specifically one's mother's sister. Also used to denote a female housekeeper or maid.

baijiu 白酒, spirits and grain-based liquors.

bian chi, bian shuo 边吃边说, "Let's continue the conversation as we eat."

biaozhun 标准, "standard." Used also to mean the standard price per head that a restaurant charges for a banquet.

bobo 伯伯, "uncle," specifically one's father's elder brother.

bomu 伯母, "aunt," specifically the wife of one's father's elder brother.

* This glossary contains only simplified characters, the nontraditional forms used in mainland China.

bugou pengyou 不够朋友, a phrase meaning "not enough of a friend."

buyao keqi 不要客气, a phrase meaning "You shouldn't be so polite," generally used to convey "You're welcome."

buzhang 部长, "minister" (government position).

changzhang 厂长, manager or director of a factory.

Chen 陈, a common Chinese surname.

chi bao le 吃饱了, to have eaten one's fill. Used at banquets to signal the host that one is satisfied.

chuzhang 处长, "division director."

dage 大哥, "eldest (or elder) brother."

dajie 大姐, "eldest (or elder) sister."

dang'an 档案, "file."

danwei 单位, "work unit."

daye 大爷, "uncle," specifically one's father's elder brother.

dongshizhang 董事长, chairman of the board of a corporation.

duo yige guanxi, duo yitiao lu 多一个关系，多一条路，a phrase meaning "One more connection offers one more road to take."

erjie 二姐, "second elder sister."

fenpei 分配, literally, "to distribute" or "apportion." To assign, as an individual to a job.

furen 夫人, an honorific title meaning "Madame"; a wife.

futuanzhang 副团长, the deputy leader of a delegation.

fuzongli 副总理, vice premier of a country.

ganbei 干杯, a phrase meaning literally "dry glass," used in toasting. "Bottoms-up."

guanxi 关系, "connections." A system of relationships and reciprocal obligations.

guanxiwang 关系网, one's relationship network.

guoyü 国语, literally, "national language." The term used to describe the Mandarin dialect in Taiwan and by many Chinese outside the mainland. Understood, but not widely used, in the PRC.

guwen 顾问, "advisor." A senior-ranking member of a delegation.

he 合, "harmony." One of the eight Confucian virtues.

hongbao 红包, a "red envelope" containing cash, given as a gift, gratuity, or bribe.

houmen 后门, the "back door." The key to delivery of products and services in China through the use of connections.

Huang 黄, a common Chinese surname.

huayü 华语, literally, "Chinese language." The term used to describe the Mandarin dialect in Southeast Asia and by many Chinese outside the mainland. Understood, but not widely used, in the PRC.

jiedai danwei 接待单位, "host organization," a Chinese unit that issues an invitation and takes responsibility for foreign guests during the time they spend in the PRC.

jingli 经理, "manager."

jüzhang 局长, "bureau director."

lao 老, "old."

laoda 老大, "eldest child."

lao'er 老二, "second-born child."

laosan 老三, "third-born child."

laowai 老外, literally, "old outsider." An affectionate term for a foreigner.

laoyao 老幺, "youngest child."

Li 李, a common Chinese surname.

li qing, renyi zhong 礼轻人意重, "The gift is trifling but the feeling is profound." The Chinese equivalent of "It's the thought that counts."

Lin 林, a common Chinese surname.

Liu 刘, a common Chinese surname.

Maotai 茅台, a 106-proof, wheat- and sorghum-based liquor frequently served at Chinese banquets.

mianzi 面子, "face." Has both the tangible and intangible meaning of the English word.

mishu 秘书, "secretary." If the person works for a high-level Chinese official, the term generally refers to a high level aide-de-camp, not a clerical worker.

nali? 哪里? an interrogative meaning "where" that is also used to deflect compliments, meaning "It was nothing."

ni hao? 你好? standard Chinese greeting meaning "How are you?"

ni naiwei? 你哪位? an expression meaning literally "Who are you?" but often used to mean "What organization do you represent?"

ni nali? 你哪里? an expression meaning literally "Where are you?" but actually used to mean "What organization do you represent?"

ni nar? 你哪儿? an expression meaning literally "Where are you?" but actually meaning "What organization do you represent?"

nüshi 女士, a title meaning "Ms."

ping 平, "peace." One of the eight Confucian virtues.

pinyin 拼音, the system of romanization of the Chinese language used in the PRC; also the Chinese word for "spelling."

putonghua 普通话, literally, "normal speech." The PRC term used to describe the Mandarin dialect.

qiang da chutou niao 枪打出头鸟, literally, "The gun shoots the bird that sticks its head out." An exhortation not to seem to be different from others.

qing yong 请用, literally, "Please use." Said by a host at the commencement of a meal to signal guests to begin eating.

qipao 旗袍, a tight-fitting, traditional Chinese dress with a high collar and long slits up the sides.

ren 仁, "benevolence." One of the eight Confucian virtues.

ru guo er wen su 入国而问俗, "If you visit a country, ask what its customs are." From *Li Ji* (*The Book of Rites*), one of the five Confucian classics.

ru jing er wen jin 入境而问禁, "If you enter a region, ask what its prohibitions are." From *Li Ji* (*The Book of Rites*), one of the five Confucian classics.

ru men er wen hui 入门而问讳, "If you cross a family's threshold, ask what its taboos are." From *Li Ji* (*The Book of Rites*), one of the five Confucian classics.

ru xiang, sui su 入乡随俗, an expression meaning literally "Enter village, follow customs." The rough equivalent of "When in Rome, do as the Romans do."

sanjie 三姐, "third eldest sister."

shengzhang 省长, governor of a province.

shifu 师傅, a form of address for waiters, store clerks, chauffeurs, hotel staff, and other tradespeople, literally meaning "master."

shizhang 市长, mayor of a city.

shushu 叔叔, "uncle."

song zhong 送终, "to attend a dying parent." A homonym of the phrase "to give a clock," and the reason clocks are not traditionally considered by the Chinese to be acceptable gifts.

suiyi 随意, a phrase meaning "at will" used during toasts to exhort someone to drink only as much as he or she wishes.

taitai 太太, an honorific title meaning "Madame"; a wife.

tie fanwan 铁饭碗, China's "iron rice bowl" incentive system of lifetime tenure in a job regardless of performance.

tong chuang yi meng同床异梦, an expression meaning "divergent interests." Its literal meaning is "two in the same bed dreaming different dreams."

tongzhi 同志, "comrade."

tuanzhang 团长, the leader of a delegation.

Wang 王, a common Chinese surname.

wei 喂, an interjection used to begin and punctuate telephone conversations.

xiansheng 先生, an honorific title meaning literally "first born," but most often used to mean "Mister" or a husband.

xiao 小, "small" or "young."

xiao 孝, "filial piety." One of the eight Confucian virtues.

xiaodi 小弟, "youngest brother."

xiaojie 小姐, an honorific title meaning "Miss"; a young, unmarried female.

xin 信, "trust." One of the eight Confucian virtues.

xiong 兄, "elder brother."

yi 义, "justice." One of the eight Confucian virtues.

Zhang 张, a common Chinese surname.

Zhao 赵, a common Chinese surname.

zhong 忠, "loyalty." One of the eight Confucian virtues.

Zhongguo tong 中国通, a "China hand." Someone with an expert understanding of China and the Chinese.

Zhongshan zhuang 中山装, a loose-fitting, high-collared jacket known popularly in the West as a Mao jacket, but actually named for Sun Yat-sen (Sun Zhongshan), the father of modern China.

zhuren 主任, "director" or "chairman."

zhuxi 主席, "chairman" or "president."

zongcai 总裁, president of a company.

zongjingli 总经理, managing director of a company.

zongli 总理, premier of a country.

zou houmen 走后门, "to enter through the back door." To obtain products and services in China through the use of connections.

Index

About the Author

A 1973 graduate of Princeton University, SCOTT D. SELIGMAN has lived in mainland China, Taiwan, and Hong Kong for more than eight of the last twenty-five years.

He was a member of the faculty of Tunghai University in Taichung, Taiwan, in the early 1970s, and following U.S. recognition of the People's Republic of China in 1979 joined the staff of the U.S.-China Business Council, a private, not-for-profit membership organization charged with promoting American trade and investment in the PRC. Mr. Seligman managed the Council's Beijing office in the early 1980s, advising American companies on China business opportunities and market entry strategies, and was a founding member of the board of governors of the American Chamber of Commerce in China.

Mr. Seligman later served the Council in Washington, D.C., as director of Development and Government Relations, and in 1985 joined the public relations firm Burson-Marsteller. He worked in the company's Washington, Chicago, Hong Kong, Taipei, Shanghai, Jakarta, and Beijing offices and was senior vice president and managing director in China for three years, ending in 1998. In that year, he joined United Technologies Corporation as director of public relations.

A native of New Jersey, Mr. Seligman is fluent in Mandarin, proficient in written Chinese, and conversational in the Cantonese dialect. He holds a master's degree from Harvard University and is the author of numerous articles on China in *The Asian Wall Street Journal* and *China Business Review.* He is also coauthor of Barron's *Chinese at a Glance,* a Mandarin Chinese phrase book/dictionary for travelers, and Barron's *Now You're Talking Chinese,* a cassette, microscript, and phrase book/dictionary kit.